WINNING CAREER MOVES

MOVES

A Complete Job Search Program
for Managers and Professionals

WINNING CAREER MOVES

A Complete Job Search Program for Managers and Professionals

Geraldine Henze

BUSINESS ONE IRWIN
Homewood, Illinois 60430

For ID, who is never far from me

This publication is designed to provide accurate and
authoritative information in regard to the subject matter
covered. It is sold with the understanding that neither the
author nor the publisher is engaged in rendering legal, accounting,
or other professional service. If legal advice or other expert
assistance is required, the services of a competent
professional person should be sought.

*From a Declaration of Principles jointly adopted by a Committee
of the American Bar Association and a Committee of Publishers.*
Sponsoring editor: Jeffrey A. Krames
Project editor: Karen J. Nelson
Production manager: Bob Lange
Designer: Jeanne M. Rivera
Art coordinator: Mark Malloy
Compositor: Eastern Composition, Inc.
Typeface: 11/13 Electra
Printer: Book Press, Inc.

Library of Congress Cataloging-in-Publication Data

Henze, Geraldine.
    Winning career moves : a complete job search program for managers
and professionals / Geraldine Henze.
        p.   cm.
    ISBN 1-55623-698-0
    1. Job hunting—United States.   2. Executives—United States.
3. Professionals—United States.   I. Title.
HF5382.75.U6H47   1992
650.14′0973—dc20   92-1079

Printed in the United States of America
1 2 3 4 5 6 7 8 9 0 BP 9 8 7 6 5 4 3 2

Preface

Winning Career Moves is for managers and professionals who, either by choice or necessity, face transitions in their work lives. Although it can benefit people entering the job market for the first time, it is written particularly with the needs of job changers in mind. According to *The 1990 What Color Is Your Parachute?* by Richard Bolles, people in the United States conduct job hunts an average of eight times during their careers, and the number is constantly rising. In fact, many vocational counselors advise clients to prepare continually for changing jobs by periodically reassessing themselves, revising their résumés, and monitoring job markets.

The need for perpetual preparedness may be unfortunate, but it is undeniably a fact of life in the United States for the foreseeable future. *Winning Career Moves* can help readers make a virtue of necessity by helping them view the unavoidable vocational changes of modern life as opportunities for coming closer to their personal visions of the good life. The first step in this process is developing a sense of your own values, preferences, and sources of happiness, which is by no means easy for most people.

To complicate matters, anxiety and anger, which mask other feelings, are apt to be the predominant feelings of anyone looking for a job, especially anyone involuntarily separated from a previous job. Rejection is part of almost every job hunt, and rejection provokes both self-doubt and anger. Add the many and varied uncertainties that accompany most job searches, and you have a truly hellish emotional brew. Thus, changing jobs represents one of the most stressful activities a person can face. When the change is involuntary—as is increasingly the case in these times of "downsizing," merging, and budget cutting—it can cause a drastic drop in self-esteem as well as financial uncertainty and social dislocation.

Yet, the search must go on, and seekers must present themselves as energetic, confident, valuable, and likable potential employees. To be helpful, any approach to job hunting must take into account the emotional realities of the hunting life and help hunters deal with the behavioral consequences of their painful emotions. *Winning Career Moves*, therefore, includes suggestions for coping with anger, anxiety, and depression and for overcoming procrastination, one of the most common and debilitating behavioral manifestations of painful or conflicting emotions.

The Socratic injunction "Know thyself" stands at the center of the value system that informs Western civilization and culture. In our own century, Freud and his followers have reasserted the importance of self-knowledge for finding happiness in both work and love. Unfortunately, however, our schools—even professional schools—do little to help us gain self-knowledge or to apply the results of self-exploration to our vocational lives. So, when facing choices about jobs and careers, few of us choose from the security of a strong sense of what we value and of what makes us happy. No single book can assure you of reaching self-knowledge, but *Winning Career Moves* can help you begin your campaign of self-discovery by guiding you through activities that will enable you to explore those aspects of your self most directly related to making choices about jobs and careers.

Though essential to making sound vocational decisions, self-knowledge alone is only one of several steps involved in securing a good job. The results of your self-exploration must find expression in the documents and conversations that lead to jobs. Therefore, *Winning Career Moves* also provides practical guidelines for constructing and distributing résumés and cover letters, using the telephone, handling interviews, and negotiating the terms of employment. It focuses on communication skills—writing, listening, speaking, and reading—because they provide the keys to both self-knowledge and persuasive self-presentation. Also, by using the time between jobs to improve your communication skills, you will be enhancing the skills required for success and personal fulfillment in managerial and professional positions.

There is no easy method of finding and following a vocational path that suits your needs as well as the economic necessities of the time and place in which you live. But searching for true vocational satisfaction, as opposed to seeking mere financial success or climbing some predefined career ladder, is one of the noblest and most challenging quests life offers. A fulfilling work life is a prerequisite to happiness, and happiness is a prerequisite to living a life of caring deeply and well for yourself and for others.

As *Winning Career Moves* made its way from proposal to completed manuscript, it benefited from the contributions of many people who generously gave of their time and magnanimously shared their experiences with me. The most important contributors have been the clients, students, and friends whose stories formed the basis of the case histories that appear throughout the book. Each case history represents a composite of many individual accounts, but none would have been possible without the frankness and openness of individuals struggling courageously and articulately through the difficult process of midlife vocational transition.

I would also like to thank several colleagues who aided me in locating sources of information and allowed me to draw on their expertise in ways that helped me formulate my own ideas more clearly: Fred Way and Elizabeth Katsivelos of the Placement Office at Columbia Business School; Bob Lear, Executive-in-Residence at Columbia Business School; Georgia Donati from the Job Information Center of the Mid-Manhattan Branch of the New York Public Library; Bruce Pennington of Pennington & Associates; Skip Stellfox of L. Marshall Stellfox & Associates; and Professor Maryann Koch of the Business School at the University of Oregon.

Last but not least, I have amassed debts of gratitude to two friends, Chris Novak and Irene Nichols, who served as intellectual sounding boards and provided emotional support throughout the writing of *Winning Career Moves*.

Geraldine Henze

Contents

Chapter One

Seven Steps to Career Success

HOW PEOPLE AND JOBS FIND EACH OTHER IN THE UNITED STATES

Who gets hired by whom to do what depends primarily on who happens to be talking to whom, when, and how. Late in 1990, Drake Beam Morin, the largest executive outplacement firm in the world, released a study of how out-of-work executives found jobs during the prior year. Of the over 1,000 executives tracked between July 1989 and July 1990, 64 percent reported finding new jobs as a result of personal contacts and networking. Fewer than 25 percent found new jobs through advertisements, headhunters, and personnel agencies combined. To be effective, your strategy for locating work must reflect these realities of how jobs and people actually find each other in the United States.

Many people approach the job market as if most openings were filled as follows. First, an organization identifies a need for new or replacement personnel. Then, through careful analysis of both current and forecasted needs, the organization creates a job description. Next, an expert in human resources, in consultation with line managers, goes over the description and determines what skills, knowledge, personal characteristics, and experience the position requires. Afterwards, a posting is created and circulated widely inside and outside of the organization so that a large number of qualified candidates learn of the opening and apply for the position. Finally, by careful weeding according to known principles, the best qualified individuals are invited for interviews and a selection is made, once again based on criteria that are well defined and against which each candidate is carefully weighed.

The above scenario accurately portrays reality in only a small number of large organizations. In most organizations, systematic selection pro-

1

cedures take a back seat to plain old "knowing the right people." The confirmation hearings for Clarence Thomas's appointment to the Supreme Court revealed just how important inside connections are in the actual hiring processes of most organizations. Even at the Equal Employment Opportunity Commission (EEOC), where we might expect jobs to be awarded based on the systematic, relatively bias-free procedures described in the above paragraph, getting work seems to depend largely on having an avenue to insiders. Mr. Thomas was selected to head the EEOC by President Bush, both of whom graduated from Yale Law School. Thomas in turn selected Anita Hill, also a Yale Law School graduate, to be his special assistant, and when he left the EEOC, his replacement was a Yale Law School graduate. Getting good work depends largely on exploiting your connections—if only because you will be competing against other job seekers exploiting theirs.

In addition, your strategy should take into account the fact that jobs are now being created most rapidly in small to midsize organizations. Smaller organizations are less likely than larger ones to have powerful personnel offices and formal policies for meeting their human resources requirements. Instead, they are more likely to depend on word-of-mouth to spread news of their personnel needs and to depend on personal recommendations in selecting from a field of candidates.

Your strategy for finding work should reflect the fact that matching people and jobs is a far-from systematic process in the United States and that the most desirable positions go to searchers who have established relationships with people inside targeted organizations. The better able you are to establish yourself as a known quantity who will fit well with other employees of an organization, the more likely you are to be chosen to fill an opening or to work on a project.

Simply finding out which organizations have needs that you can fill often requires inside information—contacts with people who know a target organization well enough to help you identify problems that you could help the organization solve or opportunities that you could help it exploit. People with this kind of inside information may be vendors, clients, competitors, or government officials with regulatory responsibilities, as well as people currently employed by an organization. Thus, your strategy for finding work should focus on creating opportunities to meet and talk with as many potential sources of inside information as possible.

According to authorities on hiring in the United States, only a fraction of the openings for managers and professionals ever find their way into public advertisements or listings. In fact, many vacancies are never even posted internally. What's more, many openings that are widely advertised are not really open because they are earmarked for a friend, relative, or political ally of someone with hiring authority. Organizations spend millions of dollars annually on recruiting programs, head-hunting firms, affirmative action plans, advertising of vacant positions, and training to teach managers how to select employees. With all this investment in locating and placing personnel, you might expect the process of matching people and positions to be scientific: you might think top managements have evolved a set of guidelines for objectively defining their personnel needs and determining who best suits them. Nothing could be further from the truth.

The stated criteria for selecting candidates often have little to do with the actual requirements for adequate or superior performance of the job in question. One veteran of the corporate recruiting scene described the situation this way:

> If some of the companies who list with us actually hired the kind of people they say they want in their job descriptions, they'd be mighty unhappy. Take the big companies that describe the kind of people they want as "self-motivated self-starters." Many of those companies wouldn't have the faintest notion of how to handle a self-motivated self-starter. And if they happened by mistake to hire one, he'd probably be out on his ear within six months.

Even when the criteria for selection are carefully defined and clearly relevant, organizations have difficulty determining which candidates measure up best against these criteria. At least half of the published advertisements for managerial and professional positions include "excellent written and oral communication skills" as a criterion for selection and success. Yet, few companies routinely ask for writing samples or require candidates to write something while visiting the site.

The truth is that most organizations make decisions regarding human resources in strikingly unsystematic ways. A *Wall Street Journal* article from January of 1991, for example, reported on high-tech companies issuing pink slips to engineers in one department while hunting desperately for engineers in another. The same article cited the case of a large insurance company laying off thousands of seasoned managers while having difficulty finding enough budget analysts.[1] Situations like these sug-

---

[1] G. Fuchsberg, "Despite Layoffs, Firms Find Some Jobs Hard to Fill," *The Wall Street Journal*, January 22, 1991.

gest that organizations often do a poor job of anticipating personnel needs, of finding people to meet them, and of providing current employees with the training and motivation needed to maintain productivity in rapidly changing economic circumstances.

What's more, interviews, which play a large part in most hiring decisions, introduce a vast arena for the operation of biases. In the labor market, a bias is any preference for one candidate over another based on characteristics that bear little or no relation to job performance. Sexual and gender biases, racial biases, ethnic biases, socioeconomic biases, biases against people who are overweight, biases against people who are short . . . the list seems endless because just about any difference between two people can serve as a motive for bias.

When personal interviews figure prominently in hiring decisions, personal biases also figure prominently. For example, few people would claim that height is a good predictor of managerial and professional performance. Yet, because our culture values tallness, the taller of two candidates is more likely to be chosen when interviews are a critical factor in hiring decisions. Unfortunately, the tallness bias—like many other biases—usually enters the decision-making process without the decision maker being aware of its operation. Because biases often operate below the level of awareness, their influence on decisions generally remains concealed until large numbers of decisions are analyzed using sophisticated statistical techniques.

The realities of hiring procedures in most organizations may seem troubling, but if you understand them, you will have a great advantage over more naive searchers because you can use your knowledge to formulate a search strategy that reflects reality, not wishful thinking. Your job hunt will be most successful—and least damaging to your self-esteem—if based on the following insights:

- Chance and bias play large roles in hiring decisions.

- Little is known about the requirements for competent performance in managerial and professional positions.

- Even when reasonable criteria for evaluating candidates have been identified, measuring candidates against them remains a subjective process influenced by a variety of cultural, organizational, and personal factors.

- A candidate can influence only a fraction of the variables involved in any given hiring decision.

- Relatively few jobs are widely posted or advertised, so getting a good job usually requires talking to the right people at the right times, which in turn means talking to many people many times.

- Your chances of getting a good job increase substantially if you use a variety of information sources to locate opportunities, rather than relying only on postings, advertisements, headhunters, or agencies.

- Your chances of finding good work soon are not very high if you simply ship off your credentials to a hundred or so likely places and wait for one or more of them to discover a potential fit between your abilities and its personnel needs.

FINDING WORK IN TOUGH TIMES

During economic downturns and recessions, jobs seem to be nowhere, but they are actually everywhere else. This paradox stems from the fact that downturns often signal adjustments in the economy—jobs are available during and after downturns, but not in the same sectors of the economy as before. To many job hunters, no jobs seem to be available because the available jobs correspond to different work than they have performed in the past. Since the stock market crash of October 1987, for example, people with a variety of specialties in finance have found themselves without jobs and have discovered that new jobs are hard to find in their old specialties. Likewise, the current corporate fad of *demassing*—flattening organizational hierarchies by getting rid of middle managers—is making traditional posts in general management harder to find.

These trends require job seekers to be flexible in defining their skills and in figuring out how to sell them, which makes thorough self-assessment more important than ever in the process of job hunting. Staying informed about business developments is also more important for job seekers during hard times. Your search strategy should include a plan for keeping up-to-date by regularly reading a variety of newspapers, periodicals, and books to keep abreast of business news and management fads. As I write, for example, Total Quality Management (TQM) tops the list of "in" business concepts, and people seeking work will find many executives in many organizations eagerly pursuing TQM projects. Being prepared to talk about how you could contribute to such efforts and being generally aware of what TQM signifies can give you an advantage over less aware candidates.

Gathering information diligently and using it imaginatively to develop sales pitches aimed at particular organizations will also give you a competitive advantage in slow times. The more you know, the better able you will be to identify areas of opportunity suited to your background and current career goals. One man I know—an editor who was handed a pink slip after the publisher for whom he worked was acquired by a large conglomerate—reasoned that collection letters would be needed more frequently as the economy worsened. So, he made himself an expert on this form of correspondence. By spending three weeks doing library research, gathering sample collection letters from friends, and interviewing a variety of experts on collection strategies, he was able to sell himself as a "collections consultant" to several small and mid-sized businesses. After six months as an independent consultant, he was offered a permanent position in the newly created corporate communications department of one of his clients.

His experience reveals not only the value of information used imaginatively, but also the rewards of flexibility in charting one's career course. More and more people, some by choice and others by necessity, are beginning to differentiate between paid work and permanent, full-time jobs. As traditional midlevel management jobs in traditional career paths become more scarce—a well-established trend that will probably continue for several years at least—more people will have to create a mix of consulting, part-time work, and temporary assignments to replace the more traditional jobs they have lost.

For better or worse, much of the work now available lacks the security and perks associated in the past with managerial and professional positions. But then again, the security and perks associated with many jobs have proven illusory. "Lifetime employers" like large commercial banks and big universities are laying off managers, administrators, and professionals in droves, and cost cutting has put an end to many an attractive perk. Even time-honored benefits like health insurance and pensions are falling victim to cost reduction and mismanagement. Job seekers able to perceive and adjust quickly to the ever-changing realities of the labor market will have a great advantage over people locked into the goal of getting traditional jobs and pursuing once-typical career paths.

During hard times, job seekers should also be prepared to spend more time looking for suitable work and to receive more no's before finding a suitable employer who says yes. *At the start of your search, figure on spending at least six months looking for the right career move for yourself.*

During this period, you may take on consulting jobs, part-time work, or temporary assignments to supplement your income. But plan to allow yourself at least six months to get your career going again at full speed in a direction that suits your current needs and goals. You may find a great job or launch a new business venture or establish a consulting practice in less than six months, but do not count on it. For one thing, during hard times organizations become more circumspect in making any decisions that involve spending money, which lengthens the decision-making process. For another, hard times generally mean more applicants for each opening, which lengthens the period required to separate the strong candidates from the weaker ones.

Feeling pressured financially and emotionally, some midcareer job changers rush into the first work situation that seems potentially bearable. In career decisions, however, haste can mean waste and worse. If you do not take the time to assess yourself and to research your options, you may jump, for example, into independent consulting only to discover that you hate working out of your home. Or you may end up working for an organization that reorganizes your new job out of existence within a year or two. Think of six months as the period of product development you owe yourself before reentering a competitive market. The American business community is often criticized for sacrificing long-term growth to short-term gain. Don't make the same mistake when your career is involved.

Rejection is another force that drives many job seekers to settle for less than a winning move vocationally. Studies of people in sales show that the most stressful part of selling is dealing with rejection day in and day out. When **you** are the product, a rejection feels even worse than when you are selling a product for someone else. Many job seekers, especially those who have based their self-esteem primarily on career success, find repeated rejection or nonresponse during vocational transition extremely painful. Some find the prospect of repeated no's so excruciating that they lower their career expectations primarily to hear someone say, "Yes, we believe you could do this job very well so we want to hire you." In their eagerness for affirmation, they lose sight of their goals and accept positions with little potential for longer-term satisfaction.

To avoid settling for less, plan to spend at least six months making a transition—don't start out with the probably unrealistic expectation that you will be fully reemployed in two or three months. Also, plan to hear and possibly to say "No" a great many times before finding a situation to which both you and a potential employer can enthusiastically say, "Yes!" Some salespeople handle rejections by viewing each no as a step closer to a yes. If past experience suggests they will hear 15 no's for each yes, they see generating a no as bringing them one-fifteenth of the way to a yes. Each rejection brings them closer to a sale. Cultivate this attitude in your job search.

TO PANIC OR TO PLAN?

Whatever you decide to do now, chances are you won't be doing it for the rest of your life in the same place. Most of us can expect to change jobs at least 8 to 10 times during our work lives. Active career planning, there- fore, has become a prerequisite to happiness in our society. Gone are the days—if ever there were such days—when we could passively stroll along a career path charted by the organization where we first happened to get a job. Planning of any sort takes time and requires gathering and analyzing information. To gain perspective on your life and insight about yourself, which will enable you to define different winning paths, you must take time to explore yourself. You must also take time to gather information about organizations and people and to create documents that will intro- duce you to potential employers.

But if you are like most people, you will be strongly tempted to rush into the job hunt before you have decided for which jobs you should be hunting and before you have equipped yourself properly for the mission by scouting the territory. You will feel pressured to get another job as soon as possible and may sacrifice thousands of dollars and much happi- ness in the years to come to make a few hundred dollars very soon.

Or you will have several months of severance or savings to ease your transition to a new job, but you will begin to look for that new job by answering ads and mailing broadcast letters or by consulting headhunters and employment agencies. If you near the end of your severance or sav- ings with no job offer in hand, you will panic and decide that you haven't time for nonsense like experimenting with exercises in self-exploration or taking trips to the library for research or composing targeted cover letters to individual firms.

Yet, the tighter the economy, the higher your expectations, and the longer you've been looking without generating any attractive job offers, the more critical it is to make time for systematic self-exploration, information gathering, letter writing, and phone calling. You should have a plan for getting your next job rather than waiting for the right job to come to you in the form of a newspaper ad or a call from a headhunter. The longer you've gone without a plan or without a plan that yields results, the more important it is for you to develop a plan or revise your current one.

Unfortunately, there is no magic formula or easy way to find a good job; success depends largely on working hard and working smart. Fortunately, however, in developing a job-search plan, you can take advantage of the experiences of job hunters before you and of vocational counselors who work with hundreds of job hunters. You can also employ the results of research on creativity. Getting a job is a creative activity very similar to problem solving, and humans through many ages have studied the conditions that allow creative activities to proceed fruitfully.

The first condition for fruitful creative work is to break the journey to the desired outcome into reasonable steps. If you want to travel from New York City to Florida, you must begin by envisioning the trip in stages and defining the requirements for each stage. You might not think of yourself as being engaged in a rigorous mental activity, but you will probably use words and images in several sophisticated ways as you plan your journey.

You will break the trip into stages as you think about how you will get to Florida (by plane, train, car, or other mode of transportation?) and as you realize that you must pick a more specific destination than "Florida" for your trip. You will also be breaking the journey into manageable steps as you think about getting airline tickets (which airline? how far in advance to book?) and imagine what you'll be doing in Florida to figure out whether you want to rent a car. At some point, you will also picture the weather in Florida while taking a mental inventory of your clothes so that you can decide whether to purchase new ones and pack intelligently. In addition, you may ask yourself who will feed the cat and pick up the mail while you are gone and so on.

These thoughts may pass through your mind quickly and occur in a seemingly chaotic manner, but the process of imagining your trip in manageable steps is often a prerequisite for taking a trip. Unable to imagine a trip in this way, we may lack the courage or ability to begin our travels. And if we begin, we are apt to have a rough trip or end in a place where we don't want to be.

The same is true of a job search, which is a journey from one job to another. The best way to begin the search is to think of it as a journey that you must break into manageable steps: you can't get from one job to another in one giant, magical leap. The seven steps described briefly below correspond to the steps involved in creative activities such as problem solving; they also reflect the advice of people who have studied vocational choice and people who are familiar with current hiring practices in U.S. organizations.

As an itinerary for your journey to new employment, the seven steps do not describe a straight path from one job to the next. You probably won't move smoothly from one step to the next in the order given, and you are likely to be working on several at once. Any attempt to break a fluid process into discrete, linear steps oversimplifies its reality.

Still, breaking the journey into stages, even approximate and tentative ones, will make starting your journey easier and will greatly improve your chances of reaching a desirable destination. Though you may be inclined to panic and want to take a giant leap into your next job, promise yourself to spend at least the next few hours of your job search on planning a strategy for making your next employment a winning career move.

AN OVERVIEW OF THE SEVEN-STEP APPROACH

Step 1: Explore Yourself

Self-exploration corresponds to what students of creativity term the stage of "immersion." Creativity begins when the creator becomes involved intellectually and emotionally with a project or problem. Reading, note taking, and interviewing may, for example, be the first step in creating a research report. Through these activities, the creator gathers information and becomes immersed in bringing this information to bear on a problem, product, or project.

Many people are tempted to begin a job search by revising their résumés, which may mean little more than adding a description of a current job. Relatively few people perform a thorough, systematic review of their careers as preparation for writing a résumé. Yet, this review is what immerses you in your problem or project, which is yourself and your vocational future.

Trying to revise a résumé without reviewing your career is like trying to prepare your income taxes without first reviewing your records and receipts. If you haven't reviewed your career in writing within the last three years, you should do so before trying to revise your résumé. Chapter 3 will provide more specific suggestions and exercises to guide you through the process of exploring yourself in relation to your career. Going through this process will enable you to create a stronger résumé while preparing you to identify appropriate employment objectives and to pursue them wholeheartedly.

Step 2: Define Objectives

Drawing again on the analogy of a journey, you need to have a sense of where you want to go before you can figure out a good way to get there. The self-exploration of Step 1 should provide a great deal of information about what you do well and want from life. Where you want to go will also depend on factors external to your own desires and preferences. You will need to consider economic and social trends to determine what kinds of jobs can be found (or made) where. Family and friends, too, may figure prominently in setting objectives.

You should consider both long-term and short-term objectives as you think about your destination, and you should also consider your priorities. You may have as one objective "making at least five thousand dollars more a year" in your next job. You may also have "moving to a rural area" as an objective. But you may find that you can't reach both these objectives in your next career move. If this happens, you need a way to determine which objective is more important to you now and to make a career decision that doesn't simply discard one objective to meet the other. With clear thought and careful planning, you will probably be able to reach both objectives, even though you may not be able to meet both of them in your next career move. Chapter 4 will help you identify your objectives systematically and explore alternative paths to reaching them.

Step 3: Document Your Abilities

Once you have explored yourself and set some objectives—even tentative objectives—you are ready to begin working on how to communicate your abilities and objectives to people you will meet during your journey to new employment.

A résumé generally serves as your introduction to organizations and helps you secure both informational interviews and job interviews. A résumé allows you to communicate efficiently about your abilities and objectives, and the process of constructing one helps you refine your sense of who you are and where you're headed vocationally. Chapter 6 gives guidelines for evaluating and revising this important document.

Step 4: Gather Information

Composing good cover letters to accompany your résumé will require you to start work on Step 4—gathering information about organizations and people—because the most effective cover letters sound personal and discuss your background specifically in relation to a particular organization.

Many folks shortchange the step of information gathering during job searches and career transitions. But if you research organizations, people, and trends, you will generally enjoy the job search more, generate more interviews, and have a higher ratio of offers to interviews than if you try to sell yourself to any and all buyers. A product that has some appeal to everyone will probably have great appeal to no one in particular. Trying to get a job without doing the appropriate research is like trying to sell a product without finding out about potential buyers.

Remember, too, that you aren't an inexpensive, throw-away product. You represent a long-term investment of many thousands of dollars. It pays for you to learn as much as you can about potential investors, both so that you can formulate a strong selling strategy and so that you don't sell yourself to the wrong investors. Chapter 4 suggests ways to gather and use information in your job search.

Step 5: Get Interviews

Interviews play a key role in most hiring decisions. You can't get a job offer without getting interviews. Though experts give varying opinions on how to work the averages, you should plan on generating *at most* a single job offer for every 10 to 15 initial interviews. Your actual average may be considerably higher or significantly lower, depending on your particular situation and aspirations, but you should always plan on having several interviews with several organizations before moving into a new job.

Getting 10 to 15 people to agree to see you for a half hour or more about jobs takes a considerable amount of effort. Once you have created résumés, gathered information, and written strong cover letters, you need to make plans for following up with phone calls at the appropriate times and to prepare for some preliminary interviewing over the phone. Getting interviews depends not only on how well you perform the first four steps, but also on how well you manage the process of distributing your credentials and following up on them afterwards. Chapter 6 helps you use correspondence and telephoning effectively to arrange interviews.

Step 6: Turn Interviews into Job Offers

Just because you can generate job interviews doesn't mean you will receive job offers. Every good salesperson knows that there's a big difference between a curious shopper and a committed customer. In an interview, you will try to bring a shopper closer to becoming a customer while also determining to what extent you want to cultivate the particular account. You don't want to alienate unnecessarily any potential customer, but you need to allocate your resources wisely so that you put most where the potential for reward is the highest.

Remember that *who is talking to whom when and how* largely determines who is hired for what jobs. Decisions about hiring are based largely on interviews, so successful job hunters are those who do well in interviews. The interviewee can influence only a fraction of the variables that determine the outcome of a selection interview, but the variables he or she can influence are very important.

Many people find interviewing to be the most anxiety-laden aspect of vocational change. Preparing properly for employment interviews can help reduce anxiety and improve performance. Turning interviews into offers requires proper follow-up as well as strong self-presentation, so Chapter 7 provides guidance both on how to prepare for interviews and on how to follow up appropriately afterwards.

Step 7: Negotiate Terms

In many organizations, where you start in terms of salary, title, benefits, and grade can have a big impact on where you can go and how long it will take you to get there. It pays to negotiate a good package, but to negotiate successfully, you must again invest time in gathering information, planning a strategy, and improving your communication skills. Chapter 8 will help you determine your worth in the job market and give you pointers on how to negotiate an employment arrangement.

MANAGING YOUR SEARCH

As you search for work, you should think of yourself as a project manager. Completion of a project on time requires several skills; you must be able to:

- Define objectives operationally.
- Create a plan and modify it when necessary.
- Identify milestones and measure progress against them.
- Coordinate several activities that are proceeding at the same time.
- Manage time effectively.
- Keep the project team motivated and on track.

Defining objectives operationally.   One of the keys to reaching objectives is to define them specifically and concretely enough to provide day-to-day direction for your project. Objectives defined in this manner are what I term *operational objectives* because they guide the daily operations that result in reaching objectives.

"Finding another job" is a reasonable objective with which to start your search. But one of your first tasks as project manager will be to refine this objective. To do so, you will have to think systematically about your values, priorities, and financial needs. In addition, you will need to gather more information about the labor market so that you can define your employment objective in a manner consistent with market conditions.

Chapter 3 will guide you through activities that will help you explore yourself vocationally and provide the information base necessary for refining your employment objectives in terms of your skills, values, and preferences. Chapter 4 examines in depth the process of gathering information about the current labor market so that you can translate your skills, values, and preferences into vocational objectives consistent with the current needs of employers. Refining and redefining your objectives is a process that will continue through much of your job search as you gather more information about yourself and about current needs of potential employers.

Creating and modifying your plan.   The seven steps outlined earlier provide a skeleton plan for managing your job search. As your search proceeds, you will need to break these steps down into more specific tasks geared to your particular situation. If, for example, your objectives involve relocation, your plan will include tasks like researching employment opportunities and living conditions in other geographical areas and arranging for interviews during extended visits to target areas.

Identifying milestones and measuring progress. In addition, you will need to develop a schedule for completing specific tasks; this schedule will help you stay motivated by providing milestones against which to gauge your progress. Staying motivated can be difficult when you have no external sources of reward and you are aiming at a goal that will probably take many months to reach. Milestones provide you with opportunities to reward yourself for what you have accomplished before you have achieved your ultimate objective.

Coordinating activities. As mentioned earlier, you will often be working on activities associated with several different steps at the same time. You will, for example, gather and analyze information throughout your job search, and you will use this information to refine your vocational objectives throughout much of your job search. Meanwhile, you will need to create or update a résumé, write cover letters, make phone calls, and go out on both informational and employment interviews. You will need to keep track of your communications to make sure that you follow up on possibilities in appropriate ways at appropriate times: you can't neglect to send thank-you notes after informational interviews just because you need to write cover letters in response to help-wanted notices in this Sunday's paper.

You will need to switch hats often and rapidly as you make your vocational transition. Sometimes you will be a writer, sometimes a researcher, sometimes a traveling salesperson, and sometimes a telemarketer. Sometimes your focus will be inward, sometimes outward. Sometimes you will assume several different roles in the course of a single day. Switching among several tasks and roles without neglecting any one of them will require you to be organized and to keep good records.

One of your first tasks as project manager, therefore, will be to set up an office for yourself. If you are provided with office space and services as part of an outplacement package from a former employer, you will be a step ahead. If not, you should begin immediately to set up a work space at your home or in the home or office of a friend or relative. Having a dedicated work space is important psychologically as well as logistically.

Most people find having an office an inducement to working, even if the office is nothing more than the corner of a room equipped with a plank of plywood held up by filing cabinets from which a phone and a typewriter can be operated.

Your office should be a place that everyone with whom you live recognizes as yours alone. When using it, you should be as free from interruption by family and friends as you would be if you were working for someone else outside your home. Keep all papers and materials related to your job search in your office, and use your office for all search-related activities, including activities like reading through the business section of the newspaper. When you are not visiting organizations, plan to spend six to eight hours each day working in your office.

Equally important is to leave your search activities behind when you leave your office at the end of the day. Don't let your search spill over into every other aspect of your life. If you devoted four or five hours a week to a hobby while you were employed, continue to do so as you search for new employment. If you normally watched TV with your family for an hour or two each evening after coming home from work, keep up the practice as you conduct your search. You should not feel that you must work exclusively on getting a new job until you land one: while you are looking for paid work, you still have a life independent of your efforts to earn a living. Don't neglect it. Instead, plan for it and coordinate it with your search activities.

Managing time effectively. Developing routines and knowing when to apply them are the essence of time management. You have probably developed a number of good work routines by this point in your life, and you should bring them to your job search. For example, many people find writing easiest early in the morning and plan their days so that they can complete the bulk of their writing chores before 11 A.M. You will be writing throughout your search, beginning with writing exercises to help in the process of self-exploration and continuing as you work on your résumé, compose cover letters, and follow up with thank-you notes after interviews. The last task in your search may well be to write a letter to your future employer confirming a mutual understanding of the terms of employment. It's a good idea, therefore, to figure out in what part of the day you are most productive as a writer and to set aside this portion of each day during your search for writing tasks.

The same principle holds for telephoning. Some people like to initiate calls early in the day and return calls later in the day; some folks find the opposite timing most comfortable. While you cannot completely control when you will receive calls, it is a good idea to set aside a particular portion or portions of each day for phone work.

In managing time effectively, starting and stopping work on schedule are crucial because you need to develop the habit of working according to plan rather than according to inspiration. If you wait until you feel in the right mood to begin a task, you will probably waste a great deal of time trying to get yourself into the right mood or castigating yourself for not being in the right mood and not, therefore, working on important tasks. So, if you haven't already developed the habit of working according to schedule rather than according to mood, now is the time to do it.

Remember, however, that stopping work on time is just as important as beginning work on time. Many people recognize the importance of starting on schedule but neglect the equally important principle of stopping on schedule rather than according to mood. This neglect can result in what might be called temporary burn-out. If you work on a task until you drop because you are in a productive mood, chances are very high that you will pay for your productive spurt of today with a significant period of downtime tomorrow. Also, you will likely neglect other tasks and develop a backlog, which will make scheduling and coordinating your activities all the harder in the days following your period of inspiration.

In addition, starting and stopping on schedule requires less time and energy than planning each day from scratch. If you get up each morning with no plan for how you will spend your day, you will very likely spend much of it figuring out what you are in the mood to do with the rest of it. Thus, having blocks of time devoted to particular kinds of activities each day can greatly simplify your scheduling.

Keeping motivated and on track. Many creative writers and artists discipline themselves to bring their daily work to a close at a point where they have a strong sense of what comes next. Doing so enables them to stop on schedule while maintaining high motivation to return to a task the following day. Some writers report, for example, that they always quit work in the middle of a sentence. This trick allows them to leave a task knowing that they will be able to return to it later and begin working on it again with a clear sense of direction and a strong desire to work.

To take advantage of this trick, you must be sure to stop at a point where you feel relatively certain of the next step. Many of us are inclined to do precisely the opposite—to keep going as long as we are moving along smoothly and to stop when we reach an obstacle or run out of energy. This latter approach, however, makes the prospect of returning to the task quite daunting because we know we will have to begin by facing an obstacle and continue until we either reach another difficult obstacle or simply wear out.

The inclination to procrastinate is often particularly strong during periods of vocational transition. The urge to put off tasks related to getting a job or charting a new career path is strong for several reasons. First, uncertainty is a potent de-motivator for many people. Being uncertain about the results of your labors may make you less inclined to start laboring. Second, the strong emotions of anger, anxiety, and depression that often accompany job loss can distract you from looking toward the future and can paralyze your efforts to act in the present. Finally, performance anxiety can become severe and debilitating when you feel you must constantly sell yourself and, therefore, constantly risk rejection. Dealing with the urge to procrastinate is, therefore, the major motivational challenge many job seekers face.

DEALING WITH PROCRASTINATION

Procrastination more often results from anxiety than from laziness or from ignorance of time-management and self-organizing techniques. In fact, far from being lazy, many procrastinators work very hard at putting off one task by energetically engaging in another. In my case, working hard at nonessential household chores is often the symptom that alerts me to procrastination in another area. When I'm not expecting company but find myself in a cleaning frenzy, I know the time has come to figure out what task or problem my cleaning is saving me from tackling.

Because procrastination often results from anxiety, attempts to overcome procrastination by better application of time-management techniques often fail. Virtually every approach to time management I have ever come across works beautifully—as long as you consistently apply its principles. The problem is getting yourself to use the principles consistently: the barriers to doing so are almost always emotional rather than intellectual or external.

Procrastination allows us to avoid the anxious feelings we experience when doing certain tasks or facing certain problems. Our emotional "reasoning" tells us that we can avoid unpleasant feelings of anxiety by avoiding the activities that stimulate these feelings. But our emotional reasoning is short-sighted; in the long run, continued procrastination increases our anxiety and can make relatively small tasks or problems into crises or disasters. Consider the case of Shelley, who had a strong tendency to put off paying bills.

When she lost her job, Shelley's inclination to procrastinate on bill paying became even stronger than it had been while she was employed. When she had a demanding job, she told herself that she neglected bill paying because she had little time for personal chores. When she became unemployed, this excuse became untenable. Even with plenty of time, she procrastinated; in fact, her procrastination became more pronounced. It became so pronounced that her gas and electric service was terminated, and the provider required her to pay a fee for resumption as well as to supply a substantial cash deposit.

What would have been a fairly simple task—paying monthly bills— became a crisis demanding a great deal of time, energy, and money to resolve. In putting off payment of bills, Shelley had been avoiding the guilt and anxiety she felt toward the issue of managing her personal finances. An experienced and effective businesswoman, she thought she should handle her personal finances in a more business-like manner— that she should formulate a monthly budget, that she should put aside a fixed amount each month for investment, and that she should become more familiar with her investment options and their tax implications.

Bill paying reminded her of her failure to meet her own performance standards, so she procrastinated: if she put off paying bills until the last possible moment, she was forced to pay them as quickly as possible, leaving no time to address longer-term issues of personal finance. When she lost her job, she rebuked herself even more strongly for not having managed her finances effectively while employed, and she became more anxious about her current financial situation. Thus, her motivation to procrastinate became stronger, even though she had more time.

Shelley's experience exemplifies several characteristics of the procrastination response to anxiety. First, anxiety-caused procrastination often looks and feels like lack of time or laziness when it is in fact neither. Second, self-rebuke rarely motivates a procrastinator to stop putting off a task. Instead, it tends to increase performance anxiety and guilt, which often caused the procrastination to begin with. Third, procrastination can be part of a vicious cycle that starts with anxiety, moves on to poor performance due to anxiety-caused procrastination, which lowers self-esteem and increases performance anxiety, which in turn increases the inclination to procrastinate, resulting in worse performance, and so on. Fourth, procrastination has a tendency to spread to activities only peripherally related to the task, situation, or problem that originally generates the anxiety. There is no necessary connection between paying bills on time and managing one's finances more actively, but paying bills can remind one of the issue of managing personal finances and thus become a target of procrastination.

To further complicate matters, procrastination is not always bad. Sometimes it signals an unreadiness to deal with a task and gives us the time we need to prepare ourselves for completing the task successfully. Many writers, for example, will "block" at points when they don't know what they want to say next. Their blocks force them to delay writing, giving them time to do more research and thinking, which helps them determine what they want to say and allows them to overcome their blocks. At other times, putting off a task reflects a rational organization of priorities. If you put off paying bills on Friday evening because a dear friend will be in town for only that evening, your procrastination represents a reasonable decision to delay your bill paying in order to take advantage of a rare opportunity.

The first step in dealing with procrastination is to explore its possible causes and to look for behavioral patterns. If you occasionally delay your bill paying a day or two because more pressing matters arise, your procrastination is not a problem. But if you put off paying bills until you get threatening letters and phone calls month after month, your procrastination is a potentially serious problem. Not all patterns of procrastination, however, are as easy to detect as in this example because many do not have such obvious and dramatic consequences.

To identify self-defeating patterns of anxiety-driven procrastination during your job search, start keeping track of what you have done each day and compare your "Have-done" lists with your "To-do" lists. Begin each day's work with a planning session: list and rank in order of importance the things you hope to accomplish that day. At the end of the day, list the tasks you have worked on or completed.

Do not simply check off items on your to-do list. Tasks often turn out to be more time-consuming and complex than we anticipate when listing what we want to do, so checking off items may not accurately reflect what you have accomplished. Bill paying again supplies a good example. In the course of paying monthly bills, which may normally take less than an hour, you may discover a possible billing error. You will then have to check your records to verify your suspicions, after which you may have to spend time on the phone to straighten out the bill with the organization that produced it. Finally, you may need to write a letter to accompany your payment. But before you send it, you may decide to get a photocopy for your own records. So, now you must make a trip to the closest photocopying machine. By the time you complete your bill paying, you may have spent considerably more time than you anticipated, but you will also have done a good bit more work. This additional work will not be reflected by a simple check next to "pay bills" on your to-do list.

Save your lists, and after a week or two, look for patterns of procrastination by comparing your to do's with your have done's. If you find that you consistently fail to complete certain kinds of tasks while generally completing other kinds, it's time to suspect yourself of anxiety-driven procrastination. Suppose, for example, that you do a load of laundry each time "do laundry" appears on your list, but that you carry on your list "write follow-up note to Mr. X" from one day to the next for over a week. Chances are that you feel uncomfortable about writing to Mr. X or about composing follow-up letters after interviews or about writing letters in general.

Weapons for combating procrastination. The urge to procrastinate during a job search is often strongest regarding activities that require communication—making phone calls, writing letters, going to meetings, networking, and so on. Even under the best of circumstances, communicating with others involves some stress because our self-images get put on the line. When self-esteem is low—as it is for many people after losing jobs or after being rejected for positions—communication becomes more threatening and the urge to avoid it becomes stronger. At the same time, the need to communicate effectively increases. The combination of shaky self-esteem and high-performance requirements is a perfect prescription for procrastination.

If you identify patterns of procrastination in your search activities, the following suggestions can help you break out of the anxiety-procrastination cycle.

1. Schedule tasks on which you tend to procrastinate for your best time of day (or night). Suppose you tend to put off writing follow-up letters. Suppose, also, that you write best after 11 P.M., when quiet reigns in your household and the potential for interruption is low. Then, you should try scheduling your follow-up letter writing for 11 P.M. to midnight each day.

2. Break difficult tasks into smaller, less daunting steps. Instead of putting on your to-do list, "Write letter to Mr. X," give yourself a more modest task by breaking letter writing into smaller steps. For example, step one might be to brainstorm on paper and create a list of points you want to include in your letter. Step two might be to write a rough draft of the letter. Step three might be to revise and edit your rough draft, and step four might be to type your revised letter (or enter revisions to your computer). Step five might be to proofread the letter and address the envelope, and step six might be to take it to the post office for mailing. Having reformulated the task of letter writing as a series of small, readily doable steps, you will probably find the job easier to start and less frustrating to finish.

3. Reward yourself for taking steps as well as for reaching your ultimate destination. Procrastinators tend to appreciate only a finished product or task and to find little joy in the actual process of getting there. As a result, tasks often seem frustrating and unrewarding until completed, which makes starting and sticking to them a tall order requiring almost super-human self-discipline. Breaking tasks into steps as suggested above helps combat this tendency. Equally important, however, is developing the habit of rewarding yourself for taking each step. Rewards need not be extravagant or expensive to be effective: allowing yourself to make and drink a fresh cup of coffee or to take a walk or to do five minutes of stretching exercises can serve as self-reinforcing rewards for taking steps. Simply switching to a different, less taxing task can even be rewarding.

4. Rehearse and prepare for difficult tasks. One of the reasons performers rehearse is to build self-confidence. When confident of their ability to perform a task expertly, most people actually look forward to performance. Most communications can be rehearsed or prepared for in one way or another before the actual performance, and the confidence rehearsal builds can help combat the urge to procrastinate.

You can rehearse for interviews by mentally switching roles with your interviewer. Imagine yourself interviewing candidates for the position you seek: write out a list of questions you would want to ask and imagine the kinds of answers you would find most persuasive. In a sense, creating outlines and rough drafts are rehearsals for writing a final draft. You can rehearse phone calls, too. List the possible responses to your call—for example, connect with answering machine or phone-mail system; reach a secretary, receptionist, or assistant; connect with your ultimate target. Then map out your strategy for handling each possible response.

Preparation rituals—like clearing the desk before letter writing or selecting the clothes for an interview the night before—also have a calming and reassuring effect on many people. Suppose you find yourself feeling anxious the day before an interview and trying to figure out ways to put it off. Stop plotting your strategy for procrastination and start preparing for the event. Pick out the suit you want to wear; iron your best shirt or blouse; shine your shoes; pack your briefcase with résumés and anything else you might want to take to the interview; practice answering questions to your bathroom mirror; take a dry-run trip to the interview site. And don't forget to reward yourself for your preparation efforts.

5. Learn more about the origins and motives for your procrastination. If procrastination is an anxiety-avoidance tactic you employ frequently and to which you were prone before the start of your job search, make dealing with it one of the immediate objectives of your career transition. Self-exploration should be the focus of your activities during the first phase of your transition, so now is an excellent time to work on understanding your use of procrastination as an anxiety-avoidance tactic.

Jane Burka and Lenora Yuen are psychologists who have worked with many procrastinators and written extensively on the topic of procrastination. If you are a perpetual procrastinator, I strongly recommend working through their book, *Procrastination: Why You Do It, What to Do About It* (Addison-Wesley, 1983). Procrastination during a job search, however, often results from the emotional residues of job loss, rather than from a pronounced and long-standing inclination to use procrastination as a psychological tactic.

Job loss can have many potentially damaging emotional consequences. Before you can take full advantage of the seven-step strategy for vocational transition (or any other strategy), you must work through the strong emotions of job loss, using them to move your transition along. Otherwise, they will stand in your way.

Chapter Two

Surviving Terminal Emotions

If you have lost—or are about to lose—your job, you are probably angry. In fact, you are probably angry even if you left your job voluntarily, because many voluntary leavings result from a history of dissatisfaction and hostility. In all likelihood, you also feel—or soon will feel—anxious about finding a new job and about coping with termination, a process that can last a few hours or several months. In addition, you may feel uncertain of your value and doubtful of your competence. From time to time during your search for a new job, you may become depressed and despair of ever finding another good position.

You must cope with the emotional fallout of separation as part of mid-career vocational transition. In the process of working on your emotions, you can learn a great deal about yourself that will help you succeed in your next job or career. But, if you don't deal with your feelings—if you try instead to bury them in the interests of moving beyond an unpleasant experience—you may be haunted by them throughout your quest for a better work life. When loss of a job sets off a cascade of anger, anxiety, and depression, the sufferer is likely to have great difficulty performing the tasks that searching for a new job requires. Unresolved anger and constant anxiety can cripple your self-confidence and interfere with your productivity, prolonging your search and preventing you from enjoying the self-discovery and vocational exploration that lie ahead.

THE INEVITABILITY OF UNPLEASANT FEELINGS

Anger almost always accompanies termination. Because anger occurs on both sides of the termination process—those who do the firing are as often angry as those who get fired—the chances of getting through job loss without feeling anger are just about zero. Since angry displays often provoke anger in others, anger can be strong, escalating, and debilitating during and after the loss of a job.

Anger and anxiety go hand-in-hand. They are related physiologically and psychologically. The *fight-or-flight response* is a set of interrelated and complex physical changes involving many body systems that occur automatically when we feel threatened. This response prepares us for the strenuous physical requirements of fighting or fleeing. Our skeletal muscles tense, our hearts beat faster, and we breathe more rapidly; we perspire more heavily, our pupils dilate, and nonessential systems—like digestion—shut down so that resources can be directed to functions more immediately necessary for survival. If the threat provokes anger, our bodies are prepared to do battle; if the threat provokes fear or anxiety, our bodies are prepared to take flight. In either case, the state of physiological arousal is similar.

Given the physiological similarity between anger and fear, it isn't too surprising that we find psychological connections as well between these two emotional responses. We often get angry at what we fear, though we may be unaware of having both responses to a given provocation, and we often fear our own anger, especially when it is intense. Whether angry or anxious, we are apt to feel tense. A moderate amount of tension can be an enlivening sensation, but when tension threatens to become unbearable, we try to reduce it and restore to ourselves a sense of security and calm. Each of us has developed an arsenal of defenses against being overwhelmed by uncomfortable, tension-producing emotions.

One defense against such feelings is to stop having them. We can do so by sleeping, by using drugs—including alcohol and prescription drugs—by watching television, or by numbing ourselves with a variety of other narcotics and distractions. For many people, work is an effective haven from unpleasant feelings and may actually ward off anxiety about familial or intimate relationships. Thus, when deprived of employment, some people experience a surge of anxiety about many aspects of their lives, which gives them a strong motivation to find a way of turning off their anxieties. Not surprisingly, incidences of alcoholism, violence against children and spouses, and drug use tend to be significantly higher among the unemployed than among the general population, regardless of social or economic status.

Depression, too, can be triggered by job loss. Losing a job means losing the organization and people on which you have depended for survival because having a job means having an income, which in turn provides food, clothes, housing, and medical care. A job can also be the most important source of self-esteem in an adult's life. Performing a job can demonstrate competence and value, provide a role to play and a position within a hierarchy, and give each day an organizing principle, thus keeping existential questions and boredom at bay, rather like a good parent.

On the other hand, a job may feel somewhat like a bad parent: one who is too critical, intrusive, aggressive; one who withholds approval and reward, demands too much, or behaves too seductively. Whether people experience jobs as good parents, bad parents, or something in between, they can form extremely intense and dependent relationships with their bosses, their co-workers or clients, and ultimately with the organization that supplies employment.

Psychotherapists tell us that we tend to form dependent relationships with objects. The term *object* designates our private and unique mental representations of a person or a kind of relationship, as opposed to the real person or relationship that inspires our mental representations. An object, therefore, may be a vastly inaccurate image or a relatively realistic portrait. Frequently our objects are formed from potent mixtures of conscious and unconscious wishes, fears, fantasies, and residues of actual experiences. For most of us, mother is our first object, but we soon take as objects other important people in our lives, including fathers, nannies, siblings, and teachers. Organizations such as corporations, churches, schools, or government agencies, can also become objects in our psyches, and we can form dependent relationships with them.

Humans respond to the loss of an object with feelings of anxiety, anger, guilt, despondency, rejection, abandonment, and depression. Even when replacements for our lost objects are relatively easy to find, we may feel and behave as if our very existence were threatened. Psychotherapists explain our adult capacity to respond so strongly to object loss by pointing to our experience as children.

The human child depends for an extraordinarily long period on other bigger, older, more competent, and more knowledgeable humans for help in dealing with life's demands. To maintain this dependent state, which allows us to be elaborately socialized as demanded by contemporary society, we must form strong ties of affection with parents and other adults. But real people, as opposed to objects, are mortal, changing, needy, and insecure, so we create mental objects to meet our emotional needs more reliably than real people. We carry into adulthood our desire and ability to have reassuring relationships, which we can make into dependable objects. Depression is difficult to avoid after losing a job because psychologically we may have lost more than a job. We may have lost an object, which is a reassuring, anxiety-reducing part of ourselves, not something external and readily replaceable.

COPING WITH DIFFICULT EMOTIONS

The most important step toward coping with a difficult emotional reality is accepting it. Everyone feels terrible after losing a job, but many people fail to recognize and accept their painful responses. Those who deny, disguise, or misdirect strong feelings—defensive responses that can occur without our conscious awareness—are most apt to be overwhelmed by those feelings. Only what we allow our conscious minds to know and examine are we truly free to deal with in a rational, nondestructive manner.

A professor of mine kept a sign on the wall of our classroom that stated in bold, black letters, **"Feelings are facts."** A very simple statement, yet one of the most difficult to truly accept and know with the heart as well as the mind. Like tornados, rainbows, volcanos, and sunrises, feelings happen regardless of whether they're justified, deserved, legitimate, appropriate, or convenient. Struggling against our feelings is always a costly battle and often a losing one.

As you begin the process of searching for another job or source of income, start with the emotional facts of your situation. If you're angry, you're angry, and no amount of talking to yourself and others about how your former employer had no choice, given the state of the industry or the company or the world, will make the anger disappear. Nor will telling yourself that it was time to leave anyhow or trying to convince yourself that you never really liked the job anyway.

You're angry, and you're probably anxious about the future, and you may be or become depressed. In the long run, it is much better to confront these emotional facts than to try to make them disappear immediately and magically. Our feelings help us discover what we want; they are important messages to ourselves, which we disregard only at our own peril. Feelings do not tell us, however, where they come from, whether or to whom to express them, or how to behave in order to feel better. To answer these questions, we must think long and hard about ourselves and the situation we face, struggling to reach understanding, make sound decisions, and take reasonable action. But we can accomplish none of these desirable goals unless we start by accepting the raw facts of our feelings—the unpleasant and difficult ones along with the welcome ones.

FIGHTING ANGER

A wide range of thinkers, experimenters, and clinicians have studied and written about anger, and a wide range of ideas, attitudes, and prescriptions has resulted from their labors. Unfortunately, there is little agreement on the nature and value of anger or on how individuals and societies should deal with it.

Some psychologists, anthropologists, and sociologists consider anger to be a basically outmoded form of physiological response dating from the time when humans had to cope daily with physical threats to their well-being like lions, tigers, bears, or other humans encroaching on their territory. When fighting or fleeing were requirements of everyday life, says this school of thought, the physiological arousal of the fight-or-flight response helped both the species and the individual survive. Experts who adhere to this school of thought tend to look for ways to lessen the physiological and emotional arousal that accompanies anger—the arousal that in a sense *is* anger. Some psychiatrists, for example, believe that psychoactive drugs may ultimately be the best way to deal with strong, chronic feelings of anger, which they believe no longer serve the survival needs of either the individual or the species.

At the opposite extreme is the get-it-all-out-immediately-and-directly-and-candidly school of thought about anger. Experts who recommend expressing anger immediately and warmly tend to see anger that has been pent up, blocked, twisted, or misdirected as the source of a wide variety of psychological and physical problems ranging from self-loathing and guilt to headaches and cancer. Curiously, the appeal of these extreme ways of thinking about anger is the same in both cases: they appeal because they are simple and offer relatively easy solutions to the anger problems that all humans face. Unfortunately, anger is anything but simple: its origins, its interactions with other feelings, and the cultural rules that tell us how it may be expressed acceptably in different settings are quite complex and vary considerably from one individual to the next and from one context to another.

A second shortcoming of the extreme views, as well as of many views that lie in between, is that they have evolved primarily from studying either intimate and familial relationships or *street anger*—anger between strangers in urban settings. Remarkably little thought and research has focused on anger experienced in, or arising from, work settings. The tendency to disregard workplace anger reflects two facts of which those who experience such anger should be aware. First, the expression of anger is taboo in most organizations, particularly anger directed upward in the hierarchy. In fact, many people in organizations consider *feelings* of anger at work, as well as *expressions* of anger at work, indicative of personal shortcomings.

Second, those who study anger and deal with it in the clinical practice of psychotherapy generally have little or no personal experience of working within the management hierarchy of large organizations. Thus, psychiatrists, psychotherapists, and psychoanalysts often behave as if accounts of workplace dilemmas and passions were relevant to a client's emotional state only insofar as they reveal patterns that can be traced back to childhood or tensions arising from internal conflict. They typically dismiss the possibility of externally generated and maintained conflicts based in the reality of a client's current workplace circumstances.

This theoretical and clinical orientation *does* make a great deal of sense for many clients and many of their problems. The therapist's job, after all, is to help a client change him- or herself, not reality. Also, many emotional problems of the workplace *are* rooted in childhood experiences and internal conflicts: the way an individual responds to the stresses and traumas of employment within the modern organization *does* reveal patterns of emotional response set long before the start of working life, and for many clients the solution of work-related problems lies in changing long-established, personal patterns of thinking, feeling, and acting.

Still, the theoretical orientations and limited personal experiences of many therapists and counselors can—and often do—blind them to the very real and immediate emotional dilemmas faced by terminated or troubled employees struggling with anger and anxiety. Approaches to coping with anger based on the study of intimate and familial relationships fail to take into account some of the most basic realities of work relationships.

First, workplace relationships are *not* relationships among equals, and the inequalities are material, as well as psychological. In a marriage or love affair, either partner can initiate a termination, but at work, your bosses can fire you while you cannot fire your bosses. Similarly, your bosses can give you a poor performance appraisal that becomes part of your official personnel record, but in most organizations, you are not asked or allowed to formally appraise your bosses or comment on their performance for the record. What's more, the impact of a performance appraisal goes far beyond your personal emotional response—raises, bonuses, training opportunities, promotions, and a variety of other perks are linked implicitly or explicitly to your appraisal.

Second, emotional responses are the very spice of life in personal relationships: we expect and are expected to have strong feelings and to express them in personal relationships. Many couples, for example, view anger and fighting as normal, healthy aspects of their relationship, and many experts agree with their views. Not infrequently, couples report feeling most sexually aroused and satisfied when making up in bed after a battle. Yet, many of the same people report having great difficulty getting over anger-provoking incidents at the office, where there are no accepted mechanisms for releasing tensions by fighting or repairing relationships by reaffirming affectionate ties.

As noted previously, anger in particular and strong emotions in general are considered unprofessional, inappropriate, and possibly pathological within the majority of organizations. And, if having strong feelings at work is suspect, expressing them is taboo, which makes working them through to a satisfactory resolution impossible.

Third, in theory at least, most of us value honesty, sincerity, openness, trustworthiness, integrity, reliability, and sensitivity in personal relationships. We also tend to see these qualities as ends in themselves, rather than as strategic guidelines valued only to the extent that they help us achieve other, self-centered goals through our relationships. But in the workplace, qualities supporting self-promotion and survival of the organization implicitly or explicitly supersede the qualities generally valued in personal relationships. Although corporate training programs in interpersonal skills sometimes use words like *sincerity* and *integrity*, they view these qualities in workplace relationships as tactics for achieving corporate or career objectives, not as qualities valuable in themselves for relationships.

Fourth, workplace terminations are more isolating, brutal, and absolute than the terminations characteristic of personal relationships. A variety of social mechanisms serve to moderate and mediate the termination of personal relationships. Laws and legal proceedings, for example, force couples to continue relating long after a decision to separate has been reached. In addition, our legal system tries to ensure at least a modicum of fairness and reciprocity in settling disputes about custody of children and division of property.

Mutual friends and relatives may also provide conduits of communication for the warring parties in conflicted personal relationships, even when physical distance separates them. In the case of relationships terminated by death, our culture provides a variety of rituals to facilitate mourning the loss, recovering from it, and preserving a relationship with the deceased through fond memories. Funerals, wakes, memorial services, and anniversary observances help us through the trauma of a loved one's death; at the same time, these activities keep the deceased alive in memory, allowing us to maintain some emotional connection.

A terminated employee, on the other hand, is often a *persona non grata* at a former place of employment. Some organizations, fearing sabotage, theft, lowering of morale among survivors of personnel cutbacks, or violent and destructive acts, go so far as to give fired employees only a few hours' notice of termination and to ban them from returning to their offices. Furthermore, job loss carries a stigma—despite the rash of recent government layoffs and corporate downsizings—and our society still tends to blame the terminated employee for the loss of a job.

Because of the strong tendency to stigmatize victims and the strong inclination of victims to internalize blame, people who lose jobs do not enjoy the social, familial, and legal sympathy and support provided for those who lose other kinds of important relationships. For some, the shame associated with job loss is so great that they try to keep the loss secret as long as possible from as many people as possible. Not uncommon are reports of terminated employees who continue to prepare for work each morning and leave for the office in order to hide from family, friends, and neighbors the fact that they no longer have jobs. When the loss of a job is treated in this way, sorrow and anger cannot be expressed openly, and the loss cannot be mourned in a way that prepares the sufferer for self-repair and restoration.

Paradoxically, we have many laws and procedures to protect individuals from each other during divorce, but we provide little protection for individuals against large, powerful organizations during termination. The laws governing employment termination vary from state to state, but in many states an employee who has faithfully and effectively served an organization for dozens of years can be let go without cause, explanation,

prior notice, or severance benefits. In recent years, even the limited pro-
tections afforded by federal legislation through the Equal Employment
Opportunity Commission (EEOC) have been eroded by unfavorable
court rulings and by highly placed government appointees basically hostile to the aims of the legislation. Thus, when an organization decides to
terminate an employee, the decision is often final: not open to negotiation, legal review, or procedures to ensure fairness and some degree of
reciprocity.

The differences between workplace relationships and personal relationships result in differences between what works in dealing with workplace anger and what works in dealing with anger in personal relationships. Open, immediate, and warm expression of anger at the workplace
is likely to be self-defeating, and in many cases of termination, the employee is given little or no opportunity to express anger directly to those
responsible. Therefore, if terminated involuntarily, you are likely to have
lots of anger with no place to go. If this anger is not to poison other
relationships or turn into self-punishment, you must find a use for it and
an outlet for the tension it generates.

Aristotle considered anger a sign of injustice. We feel angry, he suggested, when we believe we have been hurt unjustly or unnecessarily.
Similarly, Harriet Lerner, a contemporary psychologist, says that anger
"exists for a reason and always deserves our respect and attention."[1] Anger, then, can be viewed as a call to action, which is precisely what our
physiological state of arousal prepares us for. Anger alerts us to the fact
that something is threatening our physical or psychological well-being,
and it tells us that we need to do something to restore ourselves to safety or
sanity. For the terminated employee, the question is: what actions will
best serve this goal?

Expressing anger directly, immediately, openly, and warmly can have
positive results in personal relationships, where you are dealing with
someone of relatively equal power in the context of an ongoing relationship in which both parties have a stake in working out a livable resolution. But in the workplace after termination, an honest display of emotion is more likely to make matters worse for you than to improve them.
Your display of anger will not result in reconsideration of the decision to
terminate, and it may provoke retaliation in the form of bad recommen-

---

[1]Harriet Lerner, *The Dance of Danger* (New York: Harper & Row, Perennial Library, 1986), p. 4.

dations, unwillingness to help you find another job, or refusal to help you get the best termination settlement possible from top management or from the folks in "Human Resources."

So, rather than expressing your anger to those responsible for your termination, sit down with a piece of paper or tape recorder and express what you feel. Also write about what you would like to do to those whom you blame for your firing. Go ahead, say it—you'd like to kill your boss (or whomever), and you'd like it to be a long, agonizing death. Or, maybe you'd like to reverse roles and fire your boss; wouldn't it be great to see how s/he would react! For many people, the best way to do this exercise is in the form of a letter to your boss, top management, or the human resources person who conveyed the news of your termination. You might want to write several letters, one to each person involved. *Do not, however, under any circumstances send any of the letters or recordings to their targets.* Their purpose is to help you discover the depth and direction of your anger and to give it an immediate outlet that will not damage yourself or others whom you love.

In dealing with angry feelings, it is always helpful to remember that the following processes are distinct from one another, even though they may become hopelessly confused during episodes of intense anger:

1. Being angry.
2. Feeling angry—experiencing and acknowledging angry responses.
3. Interpreting angry feelings.
4. Expressing angry feelings.
5. Acting angry.
6. Taking action to reduce unpleasant levels of anger arousal.
7. Rectifying/changing situations that evoke anger.

Our feelings of anger—the physiological changes that we experience as anger—are always mediated by intellectual processes. First, we become angry (i.e., have the physiological response), and we can either acknowledge and experience the response as anger or we can deny that we are angry, a process that often occurs unconsciously and may involve masking anger with other feelings such as anxiety. If we allow ourselves to feel angry, we then interpret the anger, which often amounts to assigning blame or finding an external cause for our feelings. "I feel angry" is a fact. "I feel angry *because* you fired me" (or failed to appreciate my efforts or forgot to run the errand I requested or took by baseball glove without asking, etc.) is an interpretation of the fact of my angry feelings.

Our interpretations of angry feelings, like any interpretations, may be more or less fanciful and more or less directly related to immediate experience. "I'm angry because you're selfish and never think of anyone else's needs" is an interpretation less related to immediate experience than, "I'm angry because you forgot to pick up my clothes at the dry cleaners." How we interpret angry feelings influences the intensity and expression of those feelings.

Some interpretations may serve to reduce anger, while others can intensify it. Note that interpretations can be more or less other-directed. "I'm angry because you're selfish," interprets *my* anger exclusively in terms of *your* character. This interpretation is likely to intensify my angry feelings for several reasons. First, it blames you for my anger, thus increasing my sense of having been treated unfairly or unjustly. Second, it evokes anger past and anger yet to come because it involves more than the immediate provocation of the forgotten laundry. Third, it places control of my angry feelings in your behavior, character, and attitudes—particularly in your character and attitudes—over which I have relatively little power.

If I'm angry because you're selfish, I'm doomed to unpleasant feelings of anger until you change radically. Even if you behave differently or in a way that corrects the original wrong (by, for example, immediately returning to the dry cleaners and fetching my clothes), I'm bound to continue feeling angry because your selfish attitude and character haven't changed. Finally, anger is likely to escalate because my expression of anger, based on my interpretation of feeling angry, blames you and will in many cases provoke you to anger in response.

When as part of my expression of anger I act angry, staging a display of angry behaviors such as shouting, aggressive gesturing, using strong language, and calling you nasty names, the result is often that I increase my own physiological arousal, while triggering in you an increased physiological response. The more threatening my behavior—my act—the more physiologically aroused you become in preparation to fight or flee. Thus commences what psychologist Harriet Lerner calls "the dance of anger." And as she points out, dances of anger can go on indefinitely, serving primarily to maintain the status quo in relationships. You forget my dry cleaning; I get angry and call you a selfish bastard. You get angry, too. We scream at each other until one or both of us gives in or withdraws, and we reach a fragile truce. But the truce breaks down when you forget to fill the gas tank of my car after borrowing it, and we have another fight, replete with name-calling and shouting.

Throughout all our fighting and despite all our angry energy, we fail to change the way we relate to one another, so we effectively perpetuate the very patterns that induce so much anger. Just as there are a variety of ballroom dances, there are a variety of anger dances. For example, instead of responding to my anger by shouting back at me, you might withdraw sullenly into the next room. The steps may vary, but they still form a dance, and every dance of anger has in common the tendency to perpetuate the status quo in relationships.

Caught in relationships that evoke such anger, many people search for ways to reduce the initial feelings of anger that result in so much unpleasantness: they take action to reduce unpleasant levels of angry arousal. Drugs and distractions can numb strong feelings and provide immediate relief from unpleasant feelings; fortunately, however, they are not the only ways to reduce the physiological arousal that we find so unpleasant. Learning more about ourselves and discovering new ways to interpret our angers can serve the same purpose, as well as having additional benefits. Similarly, learning new ways to express angry feelings without necessarily acting angry (i.e., improving our communication skills) can help reduce escalating, reactive feelings of anger. Finally, we can learn new and better ways to rectify the situations in our lives that provoke anger—we can learn to use our anger in ways that alter the status quo rather than in ways that perpetuate it.

All productive approaches to anger, however, require us to start by distinguishing among (1) being angry, (2) feeling angry, (3) interpreting our angry feelings, (4) expressing anger, (5) acting angry, (6) acting to reduce angry arousal, and (7) acting to change the situations and patterns in our lives that evoke anger. One purpose of the writing exercise introduced earlier is to make a start at seeing and using these distinctions. The exercise encourages you to feel anger fully and to interpret it in any way you wish, but divorces feeling, interpreting, and expressing anger from acting angry or taking any other actions based on your anger.

No writing exercise, however, will rid you of anger. Getting in touch with your current feelings is just the first step in learning more about when and how you get angry—learning new and more helpful ways to interpret angry feelings. You'll never have a better opportunity than after losing a job to explore your responses to anger, determine how they relate to anger experienced in your family of origin, and evaluate their effectiveness in getting you what you want. In addition, writing or recording your feelings will start you on an important task that should be a major aspect of your transition to new employment—improving your communication skills.

Many people would rather die than write. A surprisingly large percentage of managers, administrators, executives, and professionals detest writing, basically because they feel extremely insecure about their ability. But writing is an almost inescapable part of finding a job—you will need to write or revise your résumé, prepare cover letters, and compose follow-up correspondence. In addition, writing is one of the most powerful tools available for conducting the self-exploration that helps you determine what you want to do next and what assets you can offer potential employers. Writing skill, along with other communication skills, is also crucial to success in most management and professional careers. So, it makes a great deal of sense to use a period of unemployment to improve your writing skill and increase the ease with which you compose.

Immediately after learning of termination, you will be inspired by strong feelings, which generally make writing easier. Use the inspiration of anger and other strong feelings to get yourself into a writing habit. Because you will be writing for your own eyes only, you need not tie yourself into knots about correctness or felicity of phrasing. Thus, you may well find yourself writing far more fluently than is usually the case. For many, such fluency is a rewarding experience that can inspire greater confidence in writing ability and in the usefulness of writing as a tool for learning more about the self, which should be your first step in making the transition to the next phase of your career.

According to Douglas LaBier, a psychiatrist who has studied extensively the emotional problems associated with modern managerial and professional careers:

> [Adaptation to the organization] can bring out the *negative side of normalcy*, like feelings of guilt over self-betrayal or of trading-off too much. These feelings underlie the rage, depression, anxiety, and escapism found among many otherwise successful careerists. All of these are psychiatric symptoms. But when found among people who do not have neurotic personalities, these symptoms represent the emotional effects of too much compromising and trading-off to get ahead, even though we do those very things to succeed and therefore be considered "normal."[2]

---

[2]Douglas LaBier, *Modern Madness* (New York: Simon & Schuster, 1989), p. 4.

Returning to a job and a career path like the one you just left may be right for you, but if you don't take time to assess your experience and calmly decide what you want next in life, you may become (or continue to be) one of those "successful careerists" LaBier describes. You will perpetually feel angry, anxious, depressed, physically ill, or guilty—in short, neurotic and tremendously unhappy—as a result of compromising too much of yourself to continue climbing a career ladder. Instead of using your anger to spin your wheels and get yourself into a rut, use your anger to learn more about yourself and to improve your communication skills: then your next job will bring you more of what you truly want from life, rather than simply more of the same.

The isolation of job termination can strengthen anger while driving it underground, out of conscious awareness. When anger goes underground, it is likely to resurface as anxiety, turn into depression, or well up in response to minor provocations from people close to you. To help avoid these outcomes, begin as soon as you learn of termination to look for ways to keep yourself out in the world, that is, for ways to prevent isolation from your feelings and from other people. Following are some suggestions for staying fruitfully active and out in the world after being done in by termination.

Join a support group for job hunters. Churches, libraries, schools, and other community organizations frequently sponsor workshops and support groups for people seeking jobs. Joining a group will give you a chance to talk about your feelings with other people in similar circumstances and to learn how others respond to termination. Also, getting out to meetings will help counteract the feelings of isolation and abandonment that often accompany termination.

Check out what your community has to offer. If it's too small to offer much, check out the town or city where you worked or the nearest metropolitan area. Bulletin boards in libraries, churches, and shopping malls often carry postings of meeting times and places and provide phone numbers for getting more information. Many support groups are free or involve only nominal fees.

Become a member of a career club. For somewhat more money, you can join a nearby branch of the Five O'Clock Club or the Forty-Plus Club. These clubs are meant specifically for midcareer people out of work. *The National Business Employment Weekly*, which is published by *The Wall Street Journal* and available at newsstands and libraries throughout the country, supplies regional listings of these clubs and their activities.

Contact the placement office of your college, university, or professional school. Many placement offices provide services to alums. These range from career planning workshops and counseling to job listings. Also see what your nearest alumni association has to offer. Now is a good time to join the association, if you haven't already, and to become active in local events if any take place near you. Networking is an important part of finding out what organizations have what kind of openings, as well as in getting your foot in the door for interviews.

Read more and spend lots of time at bookstores and libraries. Read everything you can find on the topic of anger. Harriet Lerner's *The Dance of Anger* is particularly helpful and readable. It is better at providing advice on anger in personal relationships than on workplace anger. However, you will probably feel more anger in personal relationships as a result of the stress and anger caused by losing your job, so now is a good time to learn about handling anger in all relationships. Don't be put off by the fact that it is written specifically for women; virtually every insight is as valid for men as for women.

While you're at the library looking at anger books or checking out workshops for job seekers, find out whether your library has a special collection of materials on jobs and careers. Many libraries do, and some also have librarians who are specialists in locating information relevant to finding jobs. Subsequent chapters will say more about the kinds of information you need during a thorough job search, but you might as well begin now to find out what libraries in your area can provide.

Seek a helping relationship. Helping relationships come in many varieties and prices. But most psychological helping relationships offer emotional support, expertise in defining and solving problems in relationships, and aid in changing problematic behavior through a dialog focused on you, the client. Explicit payment of money for the therapist's or counselor's time—rather than implicit exchange of emotional, communicational, material, physical, sexual, and intellectual favors—forms the basis of reciprocity between client and helper.

If at all possible, get counseling as part of your severance package and negotiate for the right to select your own counselor. Best of all, get an allowance for outplacement services that you can spend as you wish. This approach will give you the widest latitude for finding a counselor, therapist, or coach (you may want to consult all three during vocational transitions) whom you find helpful and compelling.

Join a professional organization. If you hold memberships in professional organizations or associations, maintain them; if not, learn about those in your field and join one or more of them. If you are contemplating a career change, join a professional organization in the field you are considering. Professional associations are valuable sources of information and connections for people launching new careers. *The Encyclopedia of Associations* (Detroit: Gale Research) provides a comprehensive listing of professional and trade associations in the United States and can be found in most large libraries.

Now, while you are un- or underemployed, is a good time for active participation as opposed to passive membership. When engaged in full-time jobs, many people don't have time to serve on committees, attend special functions, write for newsletters, or become involved in the administrative activities that keep professional associations going. In fact, if you are concerned about the cost of maintaining membership while unemployed, you may be able to provide services in lieu of fees.

Participate in community affairs and voluntary activities. Many people also complain of having no time for church affairs, involvement in local schools, or participation in a variety of voluntary activities while employed in a demanding professional or managerial position. Well, you no longer have that excuse! The benefits of participation are many and varied; here are some that clients have related to me:

• Tom B., a systems analyst terminated when the small firm for which he worked was purchased by a larger company, volunteered to help make and serve meals to homeless people at a local synagogue. He said it helped him feel better about himself because it demonstrated his ability to make a valuable contribution to society, a far more valuable contribution, in fact, said he, than he had been making on his former job. He continued to volunteer after securing another job.

• Nancy F., a securities broker busted from her job after the 1987 stock market crash, got her first paid consulting project as a result of helping her alma mater review its portfolio of financial holdings. Another member of the review committee was so impressed by the quality of her work that he asked her to help him review and manage his family's portfolio. Now Nancy has another brokerage job, but she was able to weather a long period of unemployment because of the financial and psychic boost provided by both paid and unpaid consulting projects.

• Marty H., who lost his position as executive vice president in a bloody corporate battle of succession when the CEO died, became a mentor to a class of sixth graders. He helped them with homework, listened when they had problems with playmates or family, arranged for field trips to companies in the region, and encouraged them when they showed special interest in a particular subject or sport. Meanwhile, as a result of these activities, Marty realized that one of the things he had most enjoyed about his former job was his role as mentor, teacher, and guide to younger managers. Instead of returning to executive life, he returned to school and is preparing to teach management to graduate students of business.

Get political. As we have seen, anger can reinforce the status quo in relationships; this is true whether they be work relationships or personal relationships. If you direct your anger about termination at the rotten boss who fired you or who failed to protect you during the organizational battles that raged when costs were being cut, you are contributing to a wasteful and brutal status quo.

You rage internally, externally, or both at your "rotten boss" as the person to blame for your termination. Perhaps you have great fun with the letter-writing exercise, pointing out to him or her numerous inconsistencies, poor judgment calls, downright incompetencies, and ethical lapses. Maybe you indulge in fantasies of revenge. One client reported to me persistent fantasies of letting the air out of the tires of every grey, 1989 Lincoln Continental she saw because her boss had driven one. Another imagined secretly tape-recording staff meetings at his ad agency and sending them to clients—expletives and snide asides about clients undeleted. Over the years, I've collected many more accounts of revenge fantasies and activities than I have room to list here.

Revenge fantasies and guerrilla activities aimed at individuals can be extremely amusing and quite clever. They can also be extremely satisfying emotionally, at least in the short run. But revenge—especially directed at individuals who are themselves caught in an oppressive corporate culture—doesn't change the status quo in any significant way. In truth, powerful organizations can more easily maintain their privileged positions versus employees when employees implicitly protect organizations from serious critical examination by blaming other individuals for corporate misdeeds.

Termination is rarely, if ever, simply a personal matter, much as we may be encouraged to view ourselves or individual bosses as the culprits. So, direct some of your anger energy toward learning more about—and becoming active in—the legal and political issues related to employment termination.

Do you know whether you live in an "at will" state? Do you know where your elected representatives stand on the issue of extending unemployment benefits? Have you ever written or called one of your elected representatives on any issue? Are the budgets of job information centers in your local libraries being cut while "your tax dollars are at work" for the third summer in a row on the same segment of interstate highway and you can't detect any improvement?

Aristotle's understanding of anger as a response to perceived injustice suggests that anger may serve an important function in society. Far from being a problematic physiological anachronism, anger may be an important safeguard of community life in a modern society increasingly dominated by huge, bureaucratic organizations. Anger alerts us to possible injustice and gives us the energy to combat it. When we are able as individuals to connect with other individuals who share a cause for anger, we can combat the sense of isolation and powerlessness that job loss often evokes.

ANXIETY

Job loss provides plenty of fuel for anxiety, a feeling that many thinkers believe to be an inevitable result of modern living to begin with. You may doubt your competence and value after being fired, and you may question your ability to continue supporting yourself and your family. You may be concerned about the impact on your career of having been terminated, even if hundreds of others were let go at the same time.

The termination process itself is often fraught with anxiety-promoting experiences: you may have spent months in a state of uncertainty about the security of your position before finally getting the axe; you may have been subjected to harrowing sessions with organizational functionaries as you tried to ensure access to the retirement funds accumulated in your name or tried to figure out the paperwork involved in extending your group health insurance benefits under the provisions of COBRA.

In some respects, anxiety is even more taboo in the workplace than anger. Anger can be a sign of power, but anxiety is always taken as a sign of weakness and self-doubt. If you doubt yourself, according to workplace logic, why should anyone else have confidence in you? This attitude toward anxiety puts the recently terminated job seeker between a very big rock and a very hard place. He or she is probably quite anxious generally at this point in life and feels anxious about letting any anxiety show in interviews. Added to which may be a sense that he or she must also hide anxiety from family and spouse, lest they become plagued by anxiety too. The inclination to dampen or bury anxious feelings thus becomes very powerful, not only because they feel unpleasant, but also because they threaten the success of efforts to find another job.

As with feelings of anger, expressing your anxieties can help you cope with them. Family members, however, may be too close to be the best audience for such disclosures. Support groups, friends, and helping relationships often provide the best listening when anxiety is the subject.

A particularly useful exercise for overcoming anxiety is to play what I think of as the "worst case game." Articulate to someone else or on paper the worst things you can imagine happening during your moments of most intense anxiety. The extreme unlikelihood or outright absurdity of some of the outcomes we fear often becomes apparent only when we force ourselves to translate general feelings of anxious discomfort into actual scenarios of what might happen if our worst fears were realized. All feelings are closely related to our thought processes, but we are often unaware of the thinking habits that contribute to our emotional responses. The goal of the worst case game is to force what are sometimes termed *automatic thoughts* out into the open so that we can examine them rationally. The following example demonstrates how articulating anxieties can help keep them within reasonable limits.

A client of mine told me she had recently misplaced a confidential, intraoffice memo and feared its getting into the wrong hands. I then asked what was the worst thing that could happen if it did. She spun an incredible tale worthy of a top-flight spy novelist. It ended in the ruin of the company for which she worked and her own ostracism from the real estate industry. When she finished her fantasy, she was silent for a few moments. Then, with no further prompting from me, a big smile spread across her face. "That's pretty ridiculous, isn't it?" she concluded with a mixture of relief and amusement.

Articulating anxieties and giving them imaginative substance can help us see that many are unrealistic and that lurking behind them may be a great deal of anger. Consider John, a 50-year-old insurance company vice president who lost his job when his oldest son was a junior in college and his two younger boys were finishing high school. He sought help when his anxiety had grown so intense that he was, in his own words, "paralyzed and unable to go on looking for jobs." He explained that he had graduated from Harvard and wanted each of his sons to have a comparable education.

"But now that I'm out of a job, all I can think about is how John Jr. may have to drop out of school and my other boys may never have a chance to attend good schools. If John Jr. has to drop out now, he'll never be able to get into medical school. He'll probably have to take some job in business like I had to after graduation to pay back my loans. That would make him miserable. Sometimes I'm afraid he'll commit suicide. Many nights I just can't get to sleep because I keep picturing him driving off a cliff. We just got him a car last year."

I asked what he made of the fact that when anxious about John Jr., he pictured the young man driving off a cliff. As John Sr. elaborated on his son, the car, and himself, it became clear that he was pretty angry at John Jr. and that the car represented advantages that the older man had not enjoyed as a youth. In addition, father John had hoped that son John would volunteer to sell the car and take a summer job to help pay for tuition. John Sr. had not voiced these hopes to his son, however, and his son had not made any spontaneous offers.

Allowing himself to articulate and to listen to his anxiety—instead of wishing it would simply go away—enabled John Sr. to hear the anger, resentment, and other feelings that anxiety had been masking. Hearing them, he was able to articulate to himself and eventually to his son what he wanted John Jr. to do. Also, when some of this anxiety began to lift, John was able to evaluate his financial situation in a calmer, more realistic, problem-solving frame of mind. Dealing with financial difficulties straight on—instead of living in continual dread of running out of money at some vague date in the near future—in turn lessened anxiety and restored to John a sense of having control of his life.

Some people hide anxiety from themselves and others through anger, reversing the pattern examined above. Men seem particularly prone to respond with anger to situations that make them anxious, though both men and women can mask anxiety with anger. So, when angry, you should look for signs of underlying anxiety. Dreams often supply them.

Consider Kurt N. After 10 years of administrative service to a large university, his position was eliminated, victim of declining enrollments, shrinking federal funding, and decreasing contributions from alums—problems many colleges and universities face these days. Kurt believed, however, that his demise resulted primarily from his new boss, a former corporate executive who was appointed dean six months before Kurt received his walking papers. "I don't doubt that the school needed to cut costs—God knows, it wasted enough money!—but that bastard cut *me* because I wouldn't suck up to him like his ass-licking subordinates in the corporate world."

One night, Kurt even dreamed about "the bastard." His dream featured a single scenario repeated in several offices. In each office, Kurt was having an interview that he thought was going quite well. But time and time again, his interviewer turned into his former boss and began to attack him. After a bloody physical battle, Kurt escaped each time to find himself facing the same plight in a new setting. As he recounted this dream, Kurt seemed to work himself into a rage. He reported that while dreaming he had tried to wake himself up several times and that when he finally did awake, he found himself sweating and shaking. His dream was clearly suffused with anxiety, even though angry feelings were just as clearly dominant during the retelling.

As Kurt talked about his dream and the thoughts it brought to mind, his anxieties began to emerge more articulately. For several months prior to discharge, he had been considering a career change: he wanted to try his hand at management in the business world. His formal schooling, however, was in "higher education administration," a field in which he held a master's degree. His difficulties with his former boss—the executive turned dean—deprived him not only of his old job but also of his plans for the future. Kurt feared that no one in the business world would hire him because everyone would turn out to be like his boss, the former corporate executive.

By exploring the feelings expressed in his dream, Kurt began to see more clearly his anxieties about his competence and credentials. He feared that "corporate types" would have contempt for his background and would consider him unfit for the business world. He also feared that he sounded "too academic" and couldn't "speak business lingo" convincingly. Besides, who would hire someone "who couldn't cut it even in academia, where performance standards are notoriously low?"

As long as he saw his problem as a lousy boss who was probably representative of all bosses in the business world, Kurt was stuck with a problem he could do nothing to solve. Through examination of his anger and the anxiety underlying it in his dream, he was able to redefine his problem in a way that allowed him to see possible solutions. He enrolled for business courses conducted by local business people at his community's high school. Through them he learned more about finance, accounting, and business jargon, which increased his confidence as well as his knowledge. Meanwhile, he began revising his résumé to focus less on the academic nature of his background and more on accomplishments and skills useful in any organizational setting. Finally, he got to know some of his instructors socially and discovered that not all business people were as terrible as his former boss or as his fears. One of the instructors, in fact, referred him to a colleague who offered him a job.

The silver lining of Kurt's cloud demonstrates the value of taking emotions seriously and using them as sources of information. It also demonstrates how elusive emotions can be, even (perhaps especially) when they seem to be speaking quite loudly and clearly. The information our feelings can supply must be sought after and fought for with diligence and courage. We need to seek it from dreams and fantasies, as well as from the thoughts and feelings more immediately available–and acceptable— to our conscious minds. Finally, Kurt's experience demonstrates that thinking and feeling are intertwined, which means that changing one's patterns of thinking can help in dealing with painful and self-defeating emotions.

The tendency to mistake blaming for problem solving is one of the most common forms of confused thinking that can cause painful feelings to escalate while preventing us from taking helpful action. When something goes wrong, we often direct our cognitive efforts toward figuring out who is to blame. Then, we confuse punishing someone with solving the problem that caused things to go wrong or with finding a way to make things go right.

Kurt engaged in this kind of cognitive error when he blamed his feelings of anger and anxiety on his former boss. He engaged in a second kind of cognitive error when he generalized from his experience with one former business executive—his boss—to his likely experience with all business executives. As a result of his thinking patterns, he was drawn into a downward emotional spiral that left him feeling unhappy and powerless to do anything to improve his situation.

Blaming his boss took from Kurt the power to changes his feelings. Overgeneralizing from his experience deprived Kurt of any alternative to seeing himself as unacceptable to potential employers. All he could do was feel angry at his boss and his fate, anxious about his bleak future, and powerless to change an unacceptable situation. When he was able to switch from a blaming mode of thought to a problem-solving mode, he was able to take action. By defining his problem as a lack of knowledge about business practices and terms, Kurt was able to take appropriate remedial action, which consisted of enrolling in classes that would give him the knowledge he lacked. Taking action decreased the feelings of powerlessness that had been fueling his anxieties and anger. The less angry and anxious he felt, the better able he became to enjoy his learning adventure and profit from it. As he became happier and felt more in control of his future, he became more attractive to himself and to others, which in turn helped him land a job offer.

DEPRESSION

Feeling "down" or "blue" is part of being terminated and looking for another job. Usually such feelings pass in a matter of days or sooner. You may feel depressed after learning of termination but find that when you develop a plan for getting another position, the feeling begins to lift. Many people respond to rejections from prospective employers with mild depression but find the feeling dissipates as soon as they become reinvolved in searching. Just about everyone has developed personal strategies for dealing with mild feelings of depression that follow disappointments or setbacks in life. Some people take long walks or jog; others treat themselves to a movie with family or friends. Physical activity, intellectual challenge, and social contact are among the most common means of fighting mild depression.

Not all depressions, however, are mild. A variety of thinking patterns, life circumstances, and physiological reactions seem to determine whether a given individual in a given situation will experience mild depression or descend into a prolonged period of deepening depression. Some people appear to be more prone physiologically than others to becoming depressed and to staying that way for long periods. Both because of its severity and the physiological factors involved, deep depression is recognized as a serious disease and is often treated with drugs. Antidepressants can stop the vicious downward cycle of depression, although all involve side effects and the risk of psychological or physical habituation.

If you feel depressed for more than several days or find that you must force yourself to do anything while deriving satisfaction from nothing or sometimes think about suicide, you should consult a physician about whether antidepressant medication might be helpful in your case. One of the best ways, however, to deal with depression is to tackle it before it becomes overwhelming.

Be prepared to feel down from time to time during your transition to another job or another career. As noted above, patterns of thinking and patterns of feeling are interwoven; our thoughts affect our feelings and our feelings affect our thoughts. Certain patterns of thought are closely associated with feelings of depression, and changing these patterns can help combat depression. When depressed, people are particularly prone to several intellectual fallacies, including the following:

Overgeneralization, exaggeration, and black or white thinking. All of these thought fallacies lead us to draw extreme conclusions from scant evidence. For example, after being turned down for a job, you might find yourself thinking (saying to yourself): "I'm a lousy interviewee; I always mess up and make a fool of myself. I'll never be able to get a position in marketing because I can't even market myself."

The evidence from which these conclusions are drawn—being rejected for a particular position—simply does not support such general and extreme statements. You may have been rejected for reasons having nothing to do with your performance in the interview—perhaps another candidate simply had more experience than you and was equally personable and articulate. Even if you did perform poorly in the interview, you are not doomed to poor performance in all interviews—your interviewing performance is something that you have the power to change, if you stop thinking in black or white terms and identify the aspects of your performance that need improvement. The use of words like "always," "never," and "forever" should be a tip-off that your thinking is probably fallacious.

Selective filtering of information. Another hallmark of depressed thinking is the tendency to disregard or discard any information that might challenge dark convictions of total inadequacy or powerlessness. Drawing again on the example given above, you can conclude that you are a total failure in interviews only by disregarding the fact that you have gotten jobs and promotions in the past based in large part on your interview performance. You may also be filtering out of your thinking the fact that hiring decisions are based on a complex set of factors of which your interview performance is but one.

Labeling. The statement, "I *am* a lousy interviewee," puts a label on you and is much different from a statement like, "I didn't like the way I answered some of the questions in that interview." In a sense, labeling is a form of overgeneralization: a label sounds like a factual statement but actually goes far beyond the facts of a situation and draws from them an invalid, global conclusion. The facts are simply that you were not offered a job for which you interviewed and that in retrospect you feel you could have supplied better responses to some of the questions you were asked. These facts do not add up to the conclusion, "I am a lousy interviewee." At most, they add up to the conclusion that in the future you will be able to provide better answers to some questions because of your recent experience.

Writing out your thoughts is one of the best ways to catch yourself in the act of thinking fallaciously. When you begin to feel depressed, write out your negative thoughts and conclusions about yourself, your situation, and the world. Call yourself the worst names you can imagine and paint yourself into the bleakest future you can conjure. Then go back through what you have written and pick out all the overgeneralizations, exaggerations, black or white statements, and labels you can find. List them on one side of a sheet of paper you have divided into two columns headed respectively, "Negative Conclusions" and "Counterevidence."

Next, try to remove your intellectual filtering mechanism and list in the column entitled "Counterevidence" all of the facts and considerations that tend to refute your negative conclusions. Finally, return to the statements under the "negative conclusions" heading and recast them as more limited and helpful points. For example, instead of, "I'm a lousy interviewee," you might write, "I don't like the way I've been responding to questions about my last job. I want to come up with better ways of describing how I interacted with my boss and why I was terminated."

As you go through this exercise, you will discover two things about the majority of your negative thoughts. First, they make your future look much darker and devoid of hope than is actually the case. Second, they prevent you from identifying solvable problems and ways to compensate for actual weaknesses, thus effectively stopping you from taking actions that could make you feel better and improve your situation.

Staying active is another way to prevent depression from growing to devastating proportions. When you start to feel depressed, reread the suggestions given earlier in this chapter for staying out and active in the world during periods of unemployment. Then, formulate specific activity goals for the rest of today or for tomorrow (many people tend to feel most depressed early in the day or in the evening). Specific activity goals might be:

"Spend 2 or 3 hours at the library tomorrow looking through books and articles on interviewing skills; then write for 20 minutes about what I want to say if asked how I got along with my last boss."

"Contact local 40-Plus Club to find out about membership and meeting times."

"Make follow-up phone calls to ABC, Inc. and the XYZ Co."

Good specific activity goals for combating depression consist of limited and readily doable actions—actions you know you can complete successfully. When an action is open-ended, like looking through materials on interviewing at the library, give yourself a time limit rather than thinking in terms of going to the library and spending however much time it takes to look through everything on interviewing. When you've reached your limit, stop: don't push yourself beyond it. Instead, reward yourself for reaching your goal: do something you enjoy—take a walk, have an ice-cream cone, read a murder mystery, give yourself a leisurely bath, buy your favorite food for dinner, make yourself a fresh cup of coffee.

Finally, as with the other emotions we've been examining, depression can serve as a source of important information about yourself. Many clients, for example, report feeling mildly depressed during the search for another job, even though their searches seem to be going quite well. If a sense of lethargy and lack of enthusiasm assail you even though your search is right on track and you have not recently experienced any particular disappointments, you might be aiming for the wrong vocational target.

Midcareerists who have lost jobs with which they were at least moderately satisfied often try to find a similar position in a similar organization. They define their vocational goal as resuming their climb up the same career ladder at a different company or institution. Often, if they seek coaching or counseling, they will reject exercises or discussions aimed at self-exploration, insisting that they want or need to get a job similar to the one they lost. Frequently, they feel compelled to continue making an income equal to or better than what they were making before termination. They want to maintain their lifestyles and feel that heading in a new direction would not enable them to do so. Their psyches, however, may see things differently.

Depression for such people may be a sign of internal conflict. On the one hand, they feel pressured by a variety of internal and external forces to pursue jobs like the ones they just lost. On the other, they were not really satisfied with their former jobs. They may question (or fear allowing themselves to openly question) the value of their work or the desirability of the sacrifices they have heretofore made in the name of career advancement.

The best way to avoid a depression of this sort is to take time at the start of your job hunt to explore yourself thoroughly and to set vocational goals consistent with what you truly value and desire. Chapter 3 will guide you through this crucial aspect of finding new employment.

FOR FURTHER READING

1. *The Dance of Anger* and *Modern Madness*, cited in footnotes 1 and 2 (bottom of pages 32 and 36). Excellent for exploring the sources, expressions, and results of anger.

2. Other books on anger. *Anger, the Misunderstood Emotion* (New York: Simon & Schuster, 1989) by Carol Tavris counters the "Let it all hang out" school of thought about anger. A fascinating book that draws on a variety of sources, it is practical as well as thoughtful and well-researched. Theodore Ruben's *The Angry Book* (New York: Macmillan Publishing Company, 1969) popularizes the "let it all hang out" point of view. The book does not provide particularly helpful advice for changing angry behavior, but it presents a vivid, passionate case for direct, open, and forceful expression of anger. *The Rage Within*, by Willard Gaylin (New York: Penguin Books, 1989) makes a case for viewing anger as an anachronism. It is not a self-help book, but it is helpful in thinking about anger.

3. Books on anxiety and depression. You will find a variety of books on these topics in just about any bookstore or library. One of the best in terms of providing truly self-helpful exercises is *Feeling Good: The New Mood Therapy*, by David Burns (New York: Signet, 1980).

   Anxiety and procrastination often go hand in hand. *Procrastination: Why You Do It, What to Do About It,* by Jane Burka and Lenora Yuen can help you understand and overcome anxiety-induced procrastination during your job search and beyond.

Chapter Three

Exploring Yourself

This chapter requires working as well as reading. Peruse it to get an overview of what it contains; then work through the exercises at the end.

Of all the steps in making a vocational transition that represents a winning move, self-exploration is the one midcareerists are most likely to shortchange. The inclination to bypass self-exploration is understandable. You've already worked for a number of years, and you know a great deal about yourself vocationally. Furthermore, you've garnered valuable experience through your past work, and you've demonstrated your ability to use your knowledge and skills in particular organizational contexts and perhaps in a particular industry. Your prior experience represents a large portion of your salable portfolio of assets, and the most reasonable and lucrative step you can take next is one along the same path you've been traveling. So why start at the very beginning again, trying to figure out what path to take as if you were a callow youth right out of school? There are many compelling reasons.

First, most of us live a substantial part of our lives on autopilot. We generally feel we have no choice. To stop and consider fundamental questions about ourselves and our existence every morning would be highly inefficient—the kids would never get off to school on time; the dog would pee all over the living room rug before we got around to walking him, and we'd chronically arrive late to work—assuming, of course, that we decided to go to work after such soul-searching. Routines, schedules, habits, and webs of responsibility that connect us with others are the stuff of everyday life. Without them, each day might threaten to become a chaotic muddle.

While on autopilot, however, we are always in danger of forgetting that control of the flight plan, the destination, and the route is still in our own hands. As automated control systems have become widespread, so have stories of operators falling asleep at the controls both literally and metaphorically. Operators often fail to register signs of problems, danger, or malfunction, and they frequently fail to perceive opportunities for improving the operation. Once an important signal does penetrate consciousness, an operator may be so unaccustomed to evaluating and solving problems that he or she is intellectually and psychologically paralyzed. The same paralysis can happen in everyday lives; we sometimes call it getting into a rut—if we are still awake enough, that is, to realize we aren't simply speeding smoothly along the highway to happiness. If you have just lost or left a job, you have the perfect opportunity to examine your autopilot program and decide whether it should be revised or possibly even thrown out.

The second reason for thorough self-exploration is to prepare for self-promotion. Because you have probably taken for granted much of what you accomplished everyday at work, you may be the last person to truly understand what you have to offer. If you've held the same job for several years or have been on the same career path in the same organization, you have probably gained a great deal of knowledge and skill of which you are not explicitly aware. When I counsel midcareer job seekers, I am repeatedly amazed at how little awareness they show of some of their major strengths and assets. Many have a strong tendency to overemphasize technical knowledge and ability while omitting mention of interpersonal skills, problem-solving ability, or imagination. Sometimes they are aware of these assets but don't know how to talk about them. Sometimes they fail to mention them in interviews and documents because they assume potential employers will be wondering *whether* they can do a job, rather than *how* and *how well* they can do it. Self-exploration exercises are among the best tools for preparing to revise résumés, compose cover letters, and handle interviews.

Third, you—like many, many other people—may never have explored yourself systematically with reference to vocational decision making. If you are like most people, you wound up where you are through a complex mixture of chance, external pressure, and choice. When asked how they got started in a particular career or company, most people say something on the order of, "Through the back door" or "There happened to be an opening in the X department" or "My father (or mother) made me (or wanted me to) do it." Very few give accounts that start with a systematic exploration of values, skills, and preferences leading to information gathering and resulting in the identification of short- and long-term vocational objectives. Not, of course, that they should! Often the best way to find out what you want is to get out and explore the territory, which is how many of us start our vocational lives. But you're no longer at the beginning. You've been around and have had a chance to gather much information about yourself and about the world of work. Now your job is to retrieve this information, analyze it, and use it to your best advantage.

Fourth, the world constantly changes, as do you. Skills that may have been in great demand 10 or 15 years ago may no longer give you any particular advantage in the job market. For a time, Wall Street seemed able to devour every finance major any M.B.A. factory could turn out and still be hungry for more. Since the 1987 crash, however, the pavements have become littered with financial wizards. I was stunned to read in this morning's paper that IBM first marketed its line of personal computers only 10 years ago today (mid-August, 1991). Now, any managerial or professional résumé without some reference to personal computers is at an extreme disadvantage. Also, the world of organizations is a world of passing fancies and fads, and as they come and go, buzzwords come in and out of vogue. Silly as it may seem, you may need to revise your vocabulary more urgently than you need to update your skills. When you last looked for a job, MBO (management by objectives) may have been the password; now "Total Quality" is probably the sweet nothing more likely to win you a second date. As you explore yourself, you will also be giving yourself a chance to revise the terms in which you present yourself to potential employers.

Finally, you need to tackle the extremely difficult but crucial question of why you lost your last job. Many executives and outplacement counselors believe that people who lose managerial and professional positions fire themselves. More often than not, I suspect, this view appeals to those who espouse it primarily for self-serving reasons. It helps organizational survivors assuage their guilt and calm their own fears. Meanwhile, outplacement counselors are often paid by the organization that has done the firing, and one of their missions is to deflect anger and blame away from that organization. Yet, they raise a legitimate question: why did *you* get the axe rather than the person sitting next to you or the jerk down in purchasing who has done nothing for the past 10 years except dream up new forms and procedures for complicating the procurement process? You need to answer this question for two reasons. First, it's going to come up in one form or another repeatedly during your job search. Second, answering it may help you set goals for personal development and aid you in setting your next employment objective.

As you network and talk with potential employers, you will want to have a succinct statement of why you were terminated that presents you in a positive light. This statement must also be consistent with what potential employers may hear from your former bosses or co-workers if they solicit recommendations. As well, you need a more personal understanding of your recent termination—one that may or may not coincide with your public story—to avoid getting into another employment situation that makes you unhappy. For example, in the process of examining why they lost a position, many people discover that they had, indeed, been unhappy with the management style dominant in the organization that terminated them. This information helps them explore what kind of management approach they prefer, which in turn allows them to focus their job searches on organizations and settings in which they are more likely to find a congenial management style. Then they can genuinely, enthusiastically, and credibly pitch themselves to those targeted organizations.

In general, the more you know about yourself, your values, and your preferences, the better able you will be to sell yourself. As you learn about yourself, you will build greater commitment to your own goals and develop ways of talking about yourself that stress positive attributes and attitudes. A statement such as, "I like to have challenging but clear objectives to work toward, but once they've been defined, I work best when given latitude in figuring out how best to meet them" presents you in a much better light than a statement like, "I can't stand bosses who hang over my shoulder all the time."

TEAMING UP

As you explore yourself and take the other steps for moving up to greater satisfaction in your work life, you may want to find yourself a job-search partner. Partners keep each other motivated, cheer each other up after the setbacks inevitable in a thorough job search, brainstorm together to solve problems, use each other as proofreaders for documents, role play interviews and phone conversations with each other, and prevent each other from procrastinating. As you complete self-exploration exercises, a partner can help you see patterns and themes in your life. We bring to self-exploration many inaccurate images of ourselves that may make seeing our true selves difficult. A partner may be especially helpful if there are no job clubs and support groups in your area or if you dislike working in groups.

You can locate potential partners several ways. If others from your company were let go when you got your pink slip, consider contacting one or more of them about partnering or forming a job-search group. Professional organizations and alumni associations also provide good opportunities for locating partners. Some folks find partners through notices in the personal advertising sections of newspapers or by posting notices in nearby stationery stores or copy centers, places job seekers are likely to frequent. Don't be afraid to work with someone who has a different vocational background and different vocational aspirations. We humans have a terrible tendency to become parochial in our thinking and speaking; having to explain yourself to someone from a different background can be helpful in preparing to talk about your background and goals to the new people you will meet in your quest for new employment. It can also help you see yourself and your experience in a new light while broadening your view of the world of work.

If you decide to work with a partner, plan to meet regularly at least twice a week and view meeting times as solid commitments. When you work with someone else, you have an obligation to both yourself and your cohort, and you should view your meetings as no less compelling than, for example, appointments for job interviews. Also, converse by phone once every day to report on the day's accomplishments and discuss the next day's plans. Remember, however, that your partnership is a working relationship; try not to become inadvertent contributors to each other's procrastination through lengthy, rambling phone calls. Beware, too, of conducting mutual gripe sessions. If you find yourself and your partner dwelling on the topic of the idiotic questions you've been asked in recent interviews, steer the conversation toward the topic of how you might best handle some of those questions and why interviewers might be asking them.

Some experts frown on partnering and group work (without "expert" leadership, that is) during a job search. They feel that meeting with other people who are out of work may bring the job seeker down or fuel negative feelings. "Don't hang around with losers," said one outplacement expert recently interviewed on national TV. If you see people who are unemployed as losers, you will, indeed, have trouble benefiting from partnership or group work. That, however, won't be your major problem; your major problem will be that you see *you* as a loser for not having a job. If this is the case, your first and most important task is to revise your thinking about people who lose jobs. Read about Winston Churchill's career or Lee Iacocca's. If you are inclined to believe that the best and brightest naturally rise to the tops of organizations, reflect for a few moments on Hitler and Stalin.

THE CHRONOLOGICAL CAREER REVIEW

Memories are strange, elusive entities. Yet, to a large extent, we are what we remember of ourselves. The fuller our memories, the fuller and richer our self-conceptions. Your first self-exploration activity should be to remember (literally: put together again) your vocational life since infancy, which means recalling your career of learning and working. In completing this task, you will be creating a data base from which you will draw the information for subsequent, more analytical aspects of your self-exploration. Exercise 1 at the end of the chapter will guide you through your career review.

It may take you quite a while to complete. If you don't find yourself pausing to consult family, friends, and files, you're probably trying to go too fast. Where you begin in reconstructing your vocational history is immaterial. If you find yourself having difficulty recalling your earliest years, switch to your college years and return later to your first five years.

I know you will be tempted to gloss over your early years. In fact, you may well be wondering what possible relevance your preschool activities could have to a vocational decision at this point in your life. Lots. One of Freud's major contributions to the 20th century was his insistence that early childhood holds keys to understanding an adult's personality and characteristic responses to life's challenges. Suppose one of the major memories from your first five years is that your father forced you to take swimming lessons at age three. This fact of your personal history might throw light on your later resistance to a superior's suggestion that you enroll for some management development seminars. Recalling the early experience may help you find a pattern in your responses to people in positions of authority. Having isolated the pattern, you can evaluate your response rationally, instead of being compelled for essentially irrational reasons to resist opportunities for training and development.

Many people find themselves getting back in touch with parents, siblings, and other family members to complete the exercise or to pursue themes it uncovers. Now, perhaps for the first time in years, you have the time and motivation to truly talk with family members. You may learn much of value to you personally when you ask Dad why he thought it so important for you to begin swimming lessons at three. You may find yourself actually talking with him warmly and honestly for the first time in your life, especially if you can ask him about your childhood relationship without anger, resentment, or blaming. As long as you're talking with him, why not ask him if he ever lost a job and how he felt about it? Ask your mother and siblings, too. Their answers may help you change your life.

One client, a woman in her late 30s, began after losing her job to ask friends and members of her family whether they had ever been terminated. Much to her surprise, she found that all of them—the very successful as well as the not so successful—had at one time or another lost a job or left one under duress. After recounting these findings, she went on to say, "You know, I feel really good about myself for the first time in weeks because I had the courage to ask my family about things we had never discussed before. Now I know there are people close to me who understand what I'm going through and who'll be there for me if I need a boost."

IDENTIFYING AND DESCRIBING YOUR ACHIEVEMENTS

The second exercise at the end of this chapter will consist of identifying and describing your major accomplishments in life. In the context of self-exploration, *accomplishment* and *achievement* (terms I will use interchangeably) have no concrete, objective definitions. That is, an accomplishment or achievement is what you make it. If it feels like an accomplishment *to you* to have begun speaking in complete sentences before age two, then it's an accomplishment. Similarly, if you're proud of the fact that you overcame your fear of heights to take a skiing vacation in the Alps last year, then it's an accomplishment. *Failures* work the same way.

In this, as in all self-exploration exercises, take care not to narrow your focus to activities that are obviously related to the kind of job you think you want—or, for that matter, directly related to any sort of employment. These exercises are most helpful if completed in a spirit of playful creativity. As in all creative endeavors, quantity is the first step toward quality. Separate as far as possible the important creative process of generating material from the equally important creative process of reviewing critically what you have generated. Otherwise, you won't allow yourself the freedom to discover anything you don't already know.

REFRAMING FAILURES

As you review your career and identify your accomplishments, you will doubtless also recall some failures. These are as important as your accomplishments because they are equally rich in information about you. Don't try to forget or avoid them. Instead, spend some time with them: think about them and analyze them. In what sense did you fail? Did you fail in your own eyes, someone else's, or both? How did you respond to your failures? You're still alive; apparently none of your failures was fatal—how did you cope with them? Did you persist or did you look for alternative means of getting what you wanted? Are there any patterns in your failures—do many involve relationships? Formal education? Mastery of technology? Working with superiors? Managing others? Managing resources? Acquiring physical skills? Sticking to resolutions? Completing assignments on time?

Like Frank, you may discover that the difference between accomplishments and failures isn't always clear and that failures can often be reframed as achievements. He failed the fifth grade; at the time he was mortified, and so strong was his residual shame that, as an adult, he had never revealed his failure to anyone. After reflecting on it, however, he began to think of the experience as both an accomplishment and a failure.

He realized several things. First, his failure was in large part a protest against a restrictive educational environment. Second, it got him out of that environment: his parents sent him to a different school, in which he thrived. Third, despite his unpromising experience in the fifth grade, he had managed to graduate from college and earn two master's degrees—at worst, his failure had been a temporary setback. Last, it had resulted in a lifelong interest in educational practice and philosophy, which had inspired him to teach courses after work at a nearby community college. In all, he concluded, he was pretty proud of what he had accomplished through his failure.

Once you've generated a comprehensive list of accomplishments and failures, your next task will be to take a break. Breaks from directed thinking are as important to creativity as concentrated periods of immersion. We have all had the experience of wrestling with a task or problem for hours or days without making any progress, only to find that insights come to us in the middle of doing something else like taking a shower or doing the dinner dishes. Our minds can work on problems without our conscious, deliberate participation in the process. How they do so is still mysterious, but that they do so is incontestable. Give your mind a chance to work by itself on what you've uncovered, without your conscious intervention and shaping of the results.

From your comprehensive list of accomplishments, you will be selecting your "personal bests"—the 10 accomplishments that seem most important to you. As you make your selections, consider not only how significant each accomplishment seems by external or objective standards, but also how significant each feels to you. In your heart, you may feel prouder of having planned a successful fund-raising event for your church than of having won the best-salesperson award last year, which your head may insist is far more impressive to potential employers. Go with your heart.

For one thing, you may be wrong about what will impress potential employers; for another, what impresses others depends more on presentation than on objective reality. If you speak enthusiastically about your volunteer fund-raising work, you will leave a stronger, more positive impression on an interviewer than if you speak unenergetically about the sales award. Last, but emphatically not least, the major goal at this point is still to learn about yourself, but if you won't listen to yourself, you will be a lousy student and a worse teacher.

Fortunately, most people do best those things they most enjoy doing, and they most enjoy doing those things they do best. Thus, through identifying major accomplishments, you will also be identifying both your major vocational assets and your major sources of vocational fulfillment.

CREATING A PERSONAL BALANCE SHEET

Armed with plenty of information about your accomplishments and failures, you will be ready to create a "Personal Balance Sheet" (again, you will find full instructions for this exercise at the end of the chapter). Like a balance sheet in accounting, your personal balance sheet will include both assets and liabilities.

As you think about your assets and liabilities, bear in mind that both are context-sensitive; that is, a characteristic or preference that is a liability in one context can be an asset in another. For example, on a trading floor in an investment bank, insisting on complete and documented information before committing to a position would be a serious liability. But if you were a scholar doing research in a university setting, the same insistence could contribute substantially to your success and enhance your reputation among colleagues.

Thus, one way you can use your list of liabilities is to determine what kinds of work and which kinds of settings would make best use of your personal characteristics and preferences, even those that may have seemed like liabilities in previous jobs. You should also use your liabilities to evaluate yourself for particular positions and to prepare for particular interviews.

Suppose, for example, that you suspect your age will be a liability in the eyes of an interviewer for a given position because younger candidates will probably apply for the position and may be both cheaper and more malleable. If you have anticipated a negative response to your age—that it will be seen as a liability in a given context—you can be prepared to offer evidence of compensating characteristics.

In this example, compensating characteristics might include an ability to work well with people of all ages, as evidenced by the fact that you have gotten along well with superiors who were your chronological juniors. You might also emphasize the fact that your experience has demonstrated your ability to learn quickly and adjust quickly to new challenges. As well, you might mention that you could contribute more sooner than a less-experienced candidate and that hiring you would involve less risk than hiring someone with little or no track record. Being able to anticipate which aspects of your background and which of your characteristics may be seen as liabilities by potential employers will save you from being caught off guard in interviews and will prepare you to make a much stronger case for yourself.

As you analyze your accomplishments and failures to identify your assets and liabilities, you will probably find the same skills, characteristics, and preferences coming up again and again. This repetition in itself represents important information because it may reveal vocational themes that you have never before fully recognized or articulated.

Joanna, for example, who thought of herself as a "quant jock," discovered that over half of her major accomplishments involved preparing reports for professors or higher levels of management. Never before had it occurred to her that her ability to present quantitative analyses clearly in writing was one of her major assets or that it was an activity that she enjoyed immensely. As a result of her discovery, she began exploring positions in which her writing ability could play a primary role, rather than taking a back seat to quantitative analysis. She switched from seeking reemployment as a financial analyst to pursuing jobs with producers of technical and business books. She now heads a staff of technical editors and illustrators for a major publisher.

CLARIFYING YOUR VALUES

Much unhappiness in the workplace stems from internal conflicts involving values. Employees from the lowest levels to the highest of the corporate hierarchy may experience conflict between personal values and corporate practices. Midlevel managers and professionals are particularly prone to feeling squeezed between the demands of people in higher levels and the desires of people in lower levels. A manager who enjoys his or her role as mentor and coach to subordinates may, for example, have a hard time reconciling this role with directives from above to cut-training costs or limit merit raises.

Not infrequently, managers complain of feeling dissatisfied with their work either because they feel far removed from the actual products and services the organization creates or because they see little of real value in those products and services. A financial analyst for one of the major networks recently explained his desire to change careers this way to me:

> TV is exciting and important, right? It's a rapidly changing industry, and it's the major source of current information and entertainment for many Americans. But I spend my days sitting in front of a computer crunching numbers for reports I never see for readers I don't know. Sometimes, I don't really even know what the numbers I'm crunching represent. I have no sense of how my work contributes to the programs I watch. Frankly, I suspect that most of the work I do helps executives win corporate political battles and advance their careers.

Or, as one successful and still employed advertising executive said of her job, "How good can you really feel about your work when what you ultimately do is to push junk food to kids?"

Sometimes value conflicts arise because the requirements for climbing career ladders leave little time or energy for home, partner, or children. Many people in professional and management positions value family life, personal relationships, and community participation highly but feel forced to shortchange them in order to advance their careers or, increasingly, simply to hold on to their positions amid mergers, downsizings, and organizational restructuring.

An increasing number of managers and professionals with whom I speak on the topic of vocational satisfaction complain of feeling forced to compromise their senses of themselves in insidious ways on a daily basis. Said one,

> It's like being ground down little by little. From one day to the next, you don't notice any change, but one morning you wake up and realize half of you is gone. And for me, it seems like the better half—the part that was inquisitive, imaginative, idealistic, witty, open, and spontaneous. What's left is cynical, manipulative, and boring.

At the same time, our daily papers feature stories of widespread corruption and mismanagement in large organizations. In these stories, we can sometimes catch a glimpse of managers or professionals who tried to resist or question wrong-doing only to be fired, demoted, threatened, or subjected to the corporate equivalent of KP duty. Corruption and mismanagement are not restricted to profit-seeking corporations, either: government agencies, universities, and religious organizations have all been implicated in their share of scandals recently. Workers who remain after scandals surface often feel demoralized, guilty, and angry. Frequently, they begin to question the value of their work and feel used by their employers at the same time as feeling abused by the public or regulatory agencies.

According to Douglas LaBier, author of *Modern Madness* and a psychiatrist, conflicts of the sort described in the above paragraphs and the compromises people make within themselves to cope with the demands of work life can lead to psychiatric symptoms in normal people. Psychosomatic disorders, compulsive behavior, crippling anxiety, severe depression, and sexual perversions are among the symptoms that he has found resulting from self-abandonment in the name of career success.

To make the most of your termination, you should make it an opportunity to reexamine your values and priorities. Termination is often called "a blessing in disguise" by people who have drifted into chronic unhappiness because of value conflicts generated by their former jobs. A clearer sense of your current values will enable you to make a career move that is truly a winner for you—one that brings you closer to happiness. View the value-clarifying exercises at the end of this chapter, therefore, as one of the most important aspects of your self-exploratory efforts.

THE TERMINATION STATEMENT

After you have completed all the self-evaluation exercises, you should be ready to tackle your termination statement. Since you will have spent several days or more reviewing your career, describing your accomplishments, and listing your varied skills and personal attributes, you should have some perspective on your situation. Whatever the circumstances surrounding your termination, you should be able to see that you were not let go because you lack value.

Give yourself 15 minutes to do a free-writing exercise on why you were terminated. Stick to the free-writing guidelines introduced earlier: write quickly; do not pause to reread or correct; stop when the budgeted time is up. What you produce is for you alone to see, so be frank. You may find that 15 minutes is not enough time to say all you want to say about why you were terminated. If so, block out two or three more periods of 15 minutes each and continue writing your termination story.

The true stories behind terminations are often very complex. They may start many years before the actual termination and involve mutual, growing dissatisfaction. Or they may start with a recent and discrete event like a merger or funding cut. If your whole division or company was essentially shut down, you may have a fairly simple, brief story to tell. But if some people around you were kept and some were let go, your story must be more complex because it must account for why you received a pink slip when others did not.

At some point, you may reach the conclusion that you will never really know why you were fired. In many cases, people have to live with the reality that they will never be able to assemble a satisfying (to themselves) explanation of why they were terminated. If you feel basically mystified, consider getting in touch with your former boss and with former co-workers you respect to solicit their input. Your purpose is not to dispute the wisdom or fairness of the decision to let you go, but to gather information and insight that will help you decide about your future.

At the same time, you may be creating allies helpful during your search for another job. Some superiors prove to be quite helpful when asked for feedback and vocational advice. Others leave the country for two weeks after firings to avoid dealing with any possible consequences of their decisions or actions. If your former boss is willing to talk and you are willing to listen, discussing the reasons for your termination and soliciting advice may be one of the best steps you can take toward finding another job.

Agnes, after much soul searching, took a deep breath one day and called her former boss to ask why he had fired her. She knew he had been required by his superiors to make staff cuts, but she felt uncertain about why she had been among the terminated. She had worked for the company eight years, but she had been promoted to the position from which she had been fired less than a year before. Her new position had involved supervising and coaching other engineers. Although she had supervised clerical and technical personnel in the past, she had never before managed a staff of professionals. She thought she had been doing a reasonably good job despite her anxieties about the new management role, but termination left her uncertain. Perhaps, she thought, her former boss could help her evaluate her experience as a manager of professionals, which would be useful in deciding her next career move. He did, and it was.

He told her she was a terrific engineer and a good team member but a rather inconsistent manager. She tended to delegate work then hover over her subordinates, ready to rescue them from errors or false starts. Her praise for their work was extravagant, while her criticism seemed unclear and laced with anger, as if she had been hurt personally whenever they failed to meet her expectations, which seemed to be rather often. "Agnes, I think you have the markings of a good project manager," her boss confided. "And, if the company weren't going through such a hard time," he continued, "I'd have sent you off for a bunch of training workshops and gotten you working with a more seasoned project manager for a while. But I had to make cuts, and you were underperforming as a project manager, so I felt I had to let you go." He volunteered to provide a good recommendation, the phrasing of which they discussed and agreed upon, and he spent another half hour talking with her about her career options.

Agnes was almost ecstatic after the meeting. She came away from it with her confidence in her ability restored and with a sense of having several appealing career options from which to choose. Her superior's frank but tactful criticism of her management performance left her feeling that she could go on in project management and succeed, if she got more training in management skills or secured a position in which she could get help developing them. What really stuck in her mind, however, was the statement, "You're a terrific engineer." She loved solving engineering problems. All of her personal bests had involved solving engineering and design problems. She found working as part of a team of engineers intellectually satisfying and downright fun.

She hated managing other engineers, however. She got little satisfaction from dealing with interpersonal problems and felt deprived of the satisfaction she had formerly derived from hands-on involvement with engineering problems. She had taken a management position, she concluded, only because it was the logical next step in the career ladder for engineers at her former company. She decided to stick with what she loved and to seek an engineering job in a company that provided parallel career paths for management professionals and engineering professionals so that she could continue moving upward without moving out of the realm she truly enjoyed.

Not all stories have such nice endings, of course. Many bosses refuse to meet with terminated employees. Some who agree to meetings wind up being accusatory and hostile, which is understandable from a psychological point of view but nonetheless painful for their targets. Hurting someone by firing him or her is easier emotionally if the terminator can convince him- or herself that the injury was deserved or that the person receiving it was "bad." Quite a few terminators simply develop a boilerplate explanation and reject any requests to elaborate or to discuss the matter on a more personal level.

If you had a good relationship with your boss, feel reasonably resilient emotionally, and are able to discuss your termination without displaying hostility—even if greeted with coldness, anger, or stonewalling—try to arrange a meeting after termination. In the meeting, seek feedback on your performance, discuss what you would like to say to potential employers about the reasons for your termination, ask for vocational advice, and request names of other people who might help you get information about openings elsewhere. If you don't feel comfortable with the idea of discussing your termination dispassionately with your terminator, don't do it and don't worry. Just get on with your self-exploration and develop a termination statement on your own.

THE "PERFECT JOB" DESCRIPTION

The final task in your quest for self-knowledge will be to create a job description that represents a perfect job for you at this point in your career. Armed with this description, a compendium of personal values, an inventory of vocational assets, and a thoughtful evaluation of your liabilities, you will be ready to begin the next major step in your quest for better employment—setting satisfying yet realistic vocational objectives.

I cannot overstate the importance of taking the time and making the effort to work your way *in writing* through all the self-exploratory exercises in the next several pages. You may think you know yourself and what you want very well, or you may think that you can *think* your way through the exercises without bothering to do any writing. But I'm willing to bet your thinking is wrong if these are the thoughts now crossing your mind.

Writing reveals themes and patterns that no amount of pure thinking or talking with others can uncover. Writing also forces thoughts and feelings to become more articulate and clearer than talking to one's self or to others. Finally, writing produces a record of thought and feeling to which you can return later to refresh your memory or to chart your progress.

As you write your way through the exercises, you will not only come to know yourself better but also refine your skills as a writer—skills that are valuable in any managerial or professional capacity. In addition, you will be preparing yourself for the self-promotional tasks inseparable from job hunting: some of the phrasing you generate as you do the exercises will doubtless find use in your résumé(s), cover letters, and job-related conversations. The more carefully and thoroughly you complete the exercises, the better able you will be to anticipate and respond to questions about your background, skills, and motivation. Last but not least, the exercises will help you build commitment to a particular career move, and as your commitment grows, you will become more convincing to potential employers.

So, stop reading for a while and start writing!

The Self-Exploration Kit

Exercise 1: The Chronological Career Review
Exercise 2: Identifying Major Accomplishments
Exercise 3: Describing Major Accomplishments
Exercise 4: Creating an Inventory of Vocational Assets
Exercise 5: Preparing Personal Balance Sheets
Exercise 6: Clarifying Values
Exercise 7: Describing the Perfect Position or Occupation

Before tackling these exercises, get yourself a notebook or folder for storing the material you produce.

EXERCISE 1: CHRONOLOGICAL CAREER REVIEW

Introduction: The chronological career review (see Figure 1) provides a convenient format for recalling and recording your career of learning and labor, primarily in terms of accomplishments. This focus helps you explore what you value and what values have been stressed in your upbringing, education, and experience; as well, it prepares you for emphasizing accomplishments in job-search documents and conversations.

Objective: To create a vocational data base for use in subsequent self-exploration activities and as an aid in constructing or revising your résumé.

FIGURE 1
Career Chronology

Ages	Years	Location	School/Job	Activities	Accomplishments/Failures
1–4	Born:				
5–13					
14–17					
18–21					
22–25					

Materials: Several sheets of paper; many sharpened pencils; a ruler; previous versions of your résumé and other documents helpful in recalling dates, places, and activities; a phone for contacting family members and friends who can help you recall precollege activities, achievements, and failures.

Approximate time to complete: 3 to 30 hours, depending on your age, the number of transitions and activities in your life, the detail with which you chronicle your life, and the number of other people you decide to consult.

Method: Divide a large sheet of paper (at least 8½ × 11 inches) into columns as shown in Figure 1 (you can do this and the other exercises on a personal computer, if you prefer). The time intervals into which you divide your life are not critical; some people prefer five-year intervals, while others prefer intervals of varying lengths that correspond to major periods and transitions in their lives. You will probably recall more recent experiences in the greatest detail, so you may want to group them into shorter intervals than your earlier experiences.

You need not start this exercise with the beginning of your life—you may prefer to work from your most recent years backwards or to work in both directions from the middle of your life. If you recall little or nothing from the first 5 to 10 years of life, you might want to solicit help from family members. The following topics of discussion may be helpful in reconstructing your earliest years:

1. How was your name chosen?
2. What were your first words, and when did you utter them?
3. When did you learn to walk?
4. When did your toilet training start and how did you react to it?
5. When did you learn to write your name and who taught you?
6. When did you start school or preschool?
7. When did you start getting report cards and how were your grades?
8. Did early teachers make any memorable comments about your behavior or personality?
9. Did any significant births or deaths take place in your family during your first five years?
10. When did you learn to read and what did you like reading?
11. How much TV were you allowed to watch and what were your favorite programs?

EXERCISE 2: IDENTIFYING MAJOR ACCOMPLISHMENTS

Introduction: Knowing what you do best and most enjoy doing is important both to charting your vocational future and presenting yourself persuasively to potential employers. Most of us, however, are unaccustomed to thinking of our lives as a series of accomplishments, and few of us can rattle off our 10 major achievements. This exercise is designed to help you identify your personal bests, most of which should eventually find their way into your résumé. If most of your major accomplishments seem inappropriate for your résumé because unrelated to the positions you are seeking, it's probably time for serious rethinking of your vocational direction.

Objective: To isolate the 10 accomplishments in which you take most pride. These will figure prominently in later exercises aimed at identifying your major vocational assets and clarifying your values.

Materials: Two sheets of paper and your completed career chronology.

Approximate time to complete: 30 to 90 minutes.

Method: 1. Write "Accomplishments" at the top of a sheet of paper. Then, using your completed career chronology as your basic source, list 20 to 30 accomplishments. The more the merrier, so if you reach 30 before you reach the latest phase of your career, just keep going.

Under no circumstances, however, stop before you reach 15. If necessary, remind yourself that at some point in your life you learned to do several, if not all, of the following: walk, use the toilet, read, ride a bicycle, fill out income tax forms, open a checking account, get a credit card, buy a major appliance, write essays, take a picture, program a VCR, cook an egg, drive a car, make a bed, use a telephone, consult a phone book, vote in an election, and change a tire. No one is born knowing how to do a single one of these things (of which there are more than 15), and we haven't even touched on anything directly or exclusively related to doing a job.

2. Title your second sheet of paper, "Personal Bests," and select from your comprehensive list of accomplishments the 10 that you consider the most significant.

EXERCISE 3: DESCRIBING MAJOR ACCOMPLISHMENTS

Introduction: Your accomplishments reveal a great deal about you, but before you can mine these rich sources of self-information, you must examine them in greater detail. In this exercise you will describe your accomplishments in terms that will help you identify skills, values, preferences, and personal characteristics.

Objective: To create detailed descriptions of your accomplishments, which you will use in the next exercises to create an inventory of assets, explore your values, and describe the perfect next move in your career.

Materials: 10 sheets of paper and your list of personal bests.

Approximate time to complete: 2½ to 5 hours.

Method: At the top of each sheet of paper, write one of your top 10 accomplishments. Now, pick any one of the sheets and give yourself 15 to 30 minutes to write about that accomplishment. Use the technique of "free writing" to describe the accomplishment more fully: write as quickly as you can without rushing, don't pause to reread or correct anything you've written, and stop when you've used the time you originally budgeted. Put the sheet aside and move on to the next, proceeding in the same fashion with each major accomplishment.

Use the following questions to stimulate your thinking:

- What makes you proudest about the accomplishment?
- What obstacles did you have to overcome?
- Did you have to enlist the aid of others? If so, how did you win their cooperation?
- Describe the accomplishment as a recipe: what ingredients did it require and how did you assemble them?
- What attitudes, knowledge, personal attributes, and skills did the accomplishment require or exemplify?
- Did you compete with others striving to accomplish something similar?
- Did the accomplishment require you to take any risks?

- How much and what kind of coaching or supervision did you have as you worked toward this accomplishment? Did it seem helpful or intrusive to you? Why?
- How were you rewarded for the accomplishment?
- What did you learn from the experience?
- Describe some of the feelings you experienced along the way to this accomplishment. Were you ever fearful? Did your motivation flag at times? Did you feel euphoric at times? Did you ever despair of reaching your goal?
- How did these feelings affect your performance?
- What does this particular accomplishment demonstrate about you?

EXERCISE 4: CREATING AN INVENTORY OF VOCATIONAL ASSETS

Introduction: Your in-depth descriptions of accomplishments furnish a wealth of information about your skills, personal characteristics, and preferences in terms of rewards and interpersonal context. Exercise 4 is designed to help you extract and organize this information and to express it in terms of transferable assets—qualities meaningful in almost any position in almost any organization.

Objective: To create an inventory of assets. This inventory will help you define the perfect job for yourself at this point in your career. It will also prepare you to write and talk about yourself in terms that will be compelling to potential employers.

Materials: A sheet of paper set up as illustrated in Figure 2, the list of transferable skills provided in Figure 4, and your detailed descriptions of accomplishments.

Approximate time to complete: 2 to 4 hours.

Method: Set up a sheet as illustrated in Figure 2. Read through each of your descriptions of accomplishments and pick out the information needed to create your inventory of assets. List as you read, and don't worry about repetition: every time you come to a task that required you

FIGURE 2
Inventory of Assets

Personal Characteristics	Skills
Preferred Rewards	**Preferred Interpersonal Context**

gather and analyze statistical information, for example, note "ability to gather and analyze statistical information" in the "skills" column. Repetition supplies valuable clues about your major areas of strength and experience. Many people surprise themselves as they do this exercise precisely because of the themes revealed by repetition.

To get you started, Figure 3 shows the kinds of things you might list under each category. In addition, Figure 4 presents a collection of transferable skills to help you identify skills and characteristics that are useful in any organizational setting, from your own consulting practice to a huge, bureaucratic, multinational conglomerate.

FIGURE 3
Inventory of Assets

Personal Characteristics	Skills
Independent	Analytical
Loyal	— Define clear & realistic objectives
Sense of humor	— Solve problems
Patient	— Interpret charts & graphs
Energetic	Communications
Enthusiastic	— Write clearly
Thorough	— Explain technical concepts in
Mature	non-technical terms
	— Conduct productive meetings
	Quantitative
	— Formulate budgets & track
	expenses
	— Present information
	graphically
Preferred Rewards	**Preferred Interpersonal Context**
Praise from superiors	Frequent feedback from
Personal sense of	superiors.
accomplishment	Some work in teams/groups
Money	Manage other professionals
Promotions	Some individual work
Liking & respect of co-workers	Clear reporting relationships
Winning competitive awards	Exposure to mentors/
Chances to learn new things	role models
Variety	
More autonomy & responsibility	
More time off	

FIGURE 4
Transferable Skills

Analytical Ability

Ability to:

Concentrate	Form and test	Define objectives	Reason logically
Perceive	hypotheses	Solve problems	Identify
relationships	Gather information		assumptions
Grasp concepts	Draw conclusions		
quickly			

Communication Skills

Ability to:

Listen well	Write clearly	Speak confidently	Read and retain
Follow instructions	Give instructions	Adapt messages to	information
Speak foreign	Work in groups	different	Inspire confidence
languages		audiences	Work well with a
Conduct meetings			variety of people

Quantitative Ability

Ability to:

Work with	Interpret numerical	Read and design	Prepare forecasts
numbers	results	graphs	Work with a variety
Explain	Perform	Identify	of software and
calculations	calculations	miscalculation	hardware
Develop financial	accurately	Prepare budgets	
plans			
Keep accounting			
records			

Technical Knowledge

Ability to:

Read technical	Follow regulatory	Understand	Read blueprints
reports, manuals,	guidelines	technical terms	Explain technical
and journals		and principles	concepts

Decision-Making Ability

Ability to:

See and evaluate	Make decisions	Explain decisions	Gather relevant
alternatives	consistent with		information
Consult others	organizational		Anticipate impact
	goals		of decisions

Organizational Skills

Ability to:

Plan activities	Manage own time	Set priorities	Co-ordinate
Set and meet	Define goals	Tolerate	activities of
deadlines		interruptions	others
			Adjust to changes

FIGURE 4 (*concluded*)

Maturity and Initiative

Ability to:

Work independently	Innovate	Maintain composure	Take responsibility for decisions and results
Encourage participation	Recognize need for help	Tolerate frustrations	

Potential for Growth

Ability to:

Take reasonable risks	Learn from mistakes	Apply classroom learning to work	Set appropriate goals for own development
Persist at tough tasks	Recover from setbacks		
Recognize strengths	Identify weaknesses		

Don't worry if something you want to list does not fit neatly into a single category: list it somewhere and go on. View the four categories—personal characteristics, skills, preferred rewards, and preferred interpersonal context—flexibly. They are meant to stimulate your thinking, not to restrict your imagination. If you want to add some categories or rename the ones I've suggested, go to it.

Most of the things you list will probably be positive attributes because you are drawing from your major accomplishments. If, however, you recall some negative attributes, put them in your lists, too. At this point, you shouldn't be striving to disguise weaknesses in hopes of making yourself more marketable. Remember: you're still engaged in the process of self-exploration and discovery.

EXERCISE 5: PREPARING PERSONAL BALANCE SHEETS

Introduction: Like an accounting balance sheet, your personal balance sheet will include both assets and liabilities. In addition, it will include a column for "compensating qualities," in which you will record skills and characteristics that offset each liability you identify. This exercise should be repeated several times during your job search because it provides a good way of preparing for each selection interview. Assets and liabilities are context-sensitive: an asset in one setting may be a liability in another. A balance sheet has most meaning, therefore, in reference to a particular job in a particular organization.

At this point, however, you will be striving to create a comprehensive balance sheet that reflects your own sense of the strengths and weaknesses you have exhibited in work settings.

Objective: To identify and articulate your major vocational assets and liabilities and to become familiar with a tool useful in preparing for specific interviews.

Materials: The inventory of assets you created in the previous exercise and a sheet set up as illustrated in Figure 5. Keep your descriptions of accomplishments nearby in case you want to refer to them.

FIGURE 5
Personal Balance Sheet

Assets	Liabilities	Compensating Qualities

Approximate time to complete: 1 to 3 hours.

Method: 1. From your inventory, select 10 to 15 items that you feel represent your most valuable assets and put them in the "assets" column of your balance sheet. Next, identify characteristics and preferences that might be seen as liabilities. If, for example, you are older than many other people who will be seeking the same kinds of positions, "age" might be a liability in the eyes of many potential employers. Or, if you prefer to work alone, "impatience with group work" might be a liability in many work settings.

In generating a list of liabilities, you will probably find it helpful to consider the inverse of each personal characteristic, preferred reward, and preferred interpersonal context noted on your inventory of assets. Suppose, for example, that "novelty and opportunities to learn new things" are among your preferred rewards. The inverse might be, "dislike of routine activities," which would be a liability in a great many jobs.

2. After generating 5 to 10 potential weaknesses for the "liabilities" column, you should begin thinking about how you have compensated for them in the past or how you could compensate for them in the future. If age is a liability, for example, compensating characteristics might include an ability to work well with younger people as demonstrated by the fact that you have worked well with superiors who were your chronological juniors. Another compensating characteristic might be a breadth and depth of experience that would enable you to contribute more sooner than a younger candidate, thus justifying your higher price tag.

EXERCISE 6: CLARIFYING VALUES

Introduction: Conflicts between personal values and workplace demands can create a great deal of stress and dissatisfaction. To make a truly winning career move for yourself, your next employment must help you embody and realize your values on a daily basis. At the very least, you should seek employment that minimizes value conflicts. Your first step in doing so is to become more explicitly aware of your own values.

Objective: To identify values that should play a part in your vocational choices.

Materials: Several sheets of paper and your inventory of assets.

Approximate time to complete: 3 to 6 hours.

Method: 1. Title one sheet of paper "Operational Values." Now, refer to your inventory of assets and try to translate each entry into a value. For example, suppose you listed "Increased responsibility" in the preferred rewards section. This entry suggests that you probably value self-sufficiency and autonomy. Liking to be rewarded by being given more time off may suggest that you value highly time spent with your children; on the other hand, it might suggest that you value leisure highly. There is no simple way to accomplish the translation of preferences into values: you must use your imagination and spend some time recalling your reactions to a variety of situations.

Generate as long a list of your operational values as possible. By *operational values*, I mean the values actually reflected in your choices and activities, not those you think you ought to have.

2. Next, get a fresh sheet of paper and brainstorm with yourself. List various values that come to mind. For example, you may have been brought up to believe that charity is a virtue—a quality to be valued—even though this virtue may not have emerged as one of the values demonstrated through your accomplishments. Write down "charity." Courage might be another value that comes to mind; add it to your list. Give yourself 15 minutes to brainstorm, recording what comes to mind without stopping to evaluate or criticize your productions.

3. Devote 5 to 10 minutes of free writing to each of the questions listed below. This isn't a test—no one will take points off for failing to interpret a question properly—so simply read each question once, then write what comes to mind. These questions are meant to jog your thinking and imagination, not to evoke any specific kind of response.

- What portion of your week would you ideally like to spend on personal relationships—doing things with your spouse, children, parents, siblings or friends? Describe what you would like to do during time spent with them.
- From an ethical point of view, what services or products would you get most satisfaction from providing or making? What products or services would you feel least comfortable making or providing?
- If you could select an ideal group of people with whom to work, what would the group be like? Would it contain both men and women? Would it be racially and culturally diverse or homogeneous? Would your cohorts be well educated? Well read? Highly intelligent? Interested in sports? Active in political affairs? Reli-

giously devout? What kinds of people would you bar from your ideal group? Would you prefer competitive relationships within the group or basically collaborative interactions?

- When you were a child, what kind of person did you imagine becoming as an adult? In what respects are you now like that imaginary adult? How are you different?
- If you won a big cash prize in a lottery, what would you do with the money? How would having it change your life?
- If you could magically return to age 18, what would you want to do differently in the course of your adult life? What elements of your current life would you want to include in your second chance at life?

4. Using the results of all the exercises above, generate a list of your top 10 values.

EXERCISE 7: DESCRIBING THE PERFECT POSITION OR OCCUPATION

Introduction: You have gathered a great deal of information on what you do well, what you enjoy doing, what you value, and what kind of people you like to work with. You are probably developing a sense of how well your previous job allowed you to embody your values and use your most cherished talents. This exercise puts together everything you have learned about yourself vocationally in the previous exercises. You may, therefore, want to prepare for it by reviewing your responses to the other exercises.

Objective: To write a job description for a position that would be perfect for you at this point in your life.

Materials: Paper; you may also want to look at some detailed job descriptions if you are not already familiar with this kind of document from previous jobs. The human resources department of just about any mid-to-large-size organization can supply you with samples.

Approximate time to complete: 1 to 3 hours.

Method: 1. Identify the product or service you would like to be involved in producing and the kind of organization for which you would like to work. Here are some examples:

Product or Service	Kind of Organization
Health care	A small, private hospital
Management consulting	A large, international consulting firm
Equipment for power generation	A mid-sized, privately held company
Education	A small branch of a state university
Accounting	Own professional practice
Graphic design	A large ad agency
Financial analysis	A college or university
Financial services for entrepreneurs	A well-regarded venture capital firm

Be as specific as you can. If you know you want to do tax accounting, put that down instead of "accounting"; if you know you want exposure to a variety of accounting problems, specify "general accounting." The same is true for "kind of organization"—if you can specify a particular geographical area, do so; if you can specify a size and organizational structure, write them down, too.

2. Describe the interpersonal setting for your perfect job. Would you be part of a team? Lead a team? Both? Would you work largely on your own? To whom would you report and what kind of reporting relationship would you like to have? Would you serve as a liaison among several groups, or work exclusively within a single group? Would you manage or supervise others? How and how often would your performance be evaluated and by whom? Would you have contact with clients? Vendors? Top management? Factory workers? Colleagues? Would you like to be involved in management decisions or would you rather not be involved in organizational politics?

3. Now, focus on the physical and technological setting for your perfect job. Would you use computers? Have your own office or inhabit an open office setting? Work in a lab amid the latest electronic marvels? Would you be surrounded by activity and conversation—as on a trading floor—or by sound-absorbing carpets and hushed voices? Don't forget, by the way, that you are striving for perfection, not realism. You may know very well that the majority of financial analysts at your level work in cubicles in a sea of other, similarly enclosed people, but if you want to have a private office, put that in your description.

4. Describe what you would contribute—what you would be doing to help the organization produce its products or provide its services. This section corresponds to the part of a real job description that is usually labeled "duties and responsibilities." But think, as well, in terms of the kinds of problems you would like to tackle and the kinds of skills you would like to use in your perfect position. Be playful; that is, don't let yourself get too weighed down by reality. If you would like to spend a third of every day on the factory floor assembling cars, a third designing cars using a powerful CAD system, and the remaining third in the board room forging corporate policy, say so—it's *your* perfect job, not *theirs*. If your perfect position is self-employment or business ownership, use the "contributions" section to explore what you want to do for yourself, as opposed to what you want provided by outside contractors and professionals or by employees.

Chapter Four

Defining Objectives

You probably will not be able to find your perfect job this side of heaven. Chances are very high, however, that you can come much closer to it than you were in the position you lost or left. Many of my clients get uncomfortable at this point. In one way or another they will insist that the kind of job they should be seeking depends more on the kind of jobs currently available than on the kind of job they want. Usually, this thinking stems from two misconceptions. The first is that self-marketing means figuring out what organizations want and then "packaging" one's self to conform to their desires. The second is that jobs are like products in the grocery store—there are a finite number of prepackaged items from which to select.

Think of marketing as a combination of creating a market for the product you are offering and of creating a product for which there is a market. Consider some highly successful products—the "Slinky," the telephone, and the lightbulb, for example. None was developed as a result of surveying potential consumers to determine what kinds of household products they would be willing to buy. They were created through imagination, experimentation, thought, and hard work—not unlike yourself. Once created, they were presented to potential consumers in ways that made them desirable. No successful marketer can afford to be isolated from the needs and desires of consumers, but neither can she or he become a slave to them and still retain the ability to create unique products.

A large portion of this chapter will be devoted to sources of information about job opportunities. As you gather more information about organizations and their needs, you will find that you can locate (or create) an organization that needs what you offer and that can provide the kind of work and setting you desire, provided you have a clear idea of what you want and what assets you can offer in return.

THINKING SHORT TERM AND LONG TERM

As you begin to define vocational objectives for yourself, bear in mind that you may not be able to get where you want to go in one step. Also bear in mind that you probably won't stay in your next job forever—even if you could, you probably will not want to because you and your circumstances will doubtless change in the coming years. It pays to think simultaneously about what you want in the next year or two and what you want 5 to 10 years down the road. In this way, you can be more certain of taking steps now that will be helpful in reaching your longer-term goals, as well as in meeting your shorter-term needs.

NEGOTIATING OBJECTIVES WITH YOURSELF

In a sense, you have already defined your objective by describing your perfect job: your objective is to find a job as nearly resembling your perfect job as possible. But first, you need to check your perfect job description against your inventory of assets and your list of values. Does your perfect job involve using all or most of your assets? If not, perhaps you have not yet defined a position that would be perfect for you. Would your perfect job enable you to live in accordance with your values? Some of your values, of course, will concern the realm of home, friends, family, and community. Would your perfect position allow you the time and freedom to pursue these nonworkplace values?

You may feel, for example, that a position in the corporate finance area of a top investment bank in New York City would allow you to use the abilities you most value in yourself and contribute to the building of stronger business enterprises and ultimately a healthier economy. It would also involve working with the kind of high-energy, highly ambitious, highly intelligent people whom you enjoy. Finally, you would be well compensated and could buy an apartment, which you may feel is very important to you at this point in life. But it would also demand long hours—sometimes on short notice—and a great deal of travel. Furthermore, the requirements for advancement in such a position would probably not allow you to take a leave to have a child or to care for an aging parent.

If you have no desire for children or no desire to participate in their development *and* your parents are both dead or you wish they were and plan never to speak to them again anyway *and* your preferred mode of participation in community activities is to write out checks, you may, indeed, have identified an excellent position for yourself at this point in life. You may, on the other hand, perceive potential problems: though possibly very satisfying vocationally, such a position might interfere with your ability to realize nonworkplace goals and values. What to do? You have several options, but the important thing is that you not simply disregard the potential conflicts you have identified.

First, you might focus your information gathering on identifying the top firms that have the best provisions for family-related leave taking and that see community involvement as beneficial for both the individual and the company. Books like *The Best Companies for Women* by Baila Zeitz and Lorraine Dusky (Simon & Schuster, 1988) and *The 100 Best Companies to Work For in America* by Robert Levering, Milton Moskowitz, and Michael Katz (Addison-Wesley, 1990) can help you with this task, as can informational interviewing with past and present employees.

Second, you might consider negotiating with yourself a trade-off between conflicting sets of values. Maybe you would be willing to work for a second-tier firm, where the projects might be less exciting and the compensation more modest but where the pressure and demands would take a smaller toll on your personal life. Or maybe you would be willing (if able) to postpone some of your personal goals for 5 to 10 years while you focus on your career. If you select this option, be careful. Once you establish a pattern and start moving up a career ladder, making a change can be very difficult psychologically and financially—as you may know from your recent experience.

Third, you might decide to stick with your initial choice but to negotiate more acceptable terms with the company after you have received an offer. Often the terms of employment are more flexible than job seekers believe, especially after a company has committed itself by making an offer. Relatively few offers are simply, "Take it or get lost!"

Finally, you can focus your thinking and research on identifying positions that would give you satisfactions similar to the ones you hope to find in corporate finance (or whatever) but that would involve less compromising of your personal goals and values. Frequently, this is the most reasonable option, though it is infrequently given enough serious consideration. Ignorance about the vast diversity of the American workplace is sometimes the culprit; people's knowledge of vocational possibilities is often limited to what they have learned rather haphazardly from their own experience and that of close friends and family. Sometimes the problem is a rusty imagination—difficulty conceiving of how one might satisfy one's needs and desires in contexts different from the jobs or organizational settings with which one is familiar.

Rebecca exemplifies what I mean. She was soon going to lose her job as an account executive in a large ad agency because of a merger and the firm's loss of several large accounts. Despite her awareness that jobs in agencies were very scarce and the competition for them intense, she felt she *had* to get another position in account management at an ad agency. "What do you like so much about ad agencies and account management," I enquired. "Everything!" was her reply. "Could you be more specific—break 'everything' into some of its components?" I asked. "No," she replied swiftly with annoyance, "it's the whole gestalt, the whole feel of agency work and the kind of people who do advertising." After a few more conversational turns of this nature got us nowhere, I gave her an assignment.

She was to record the activities of her next work day in half hour intervals—what she was doing, where she was doing it, and whom she was with. Then she was to describe the people with whom she had contact—how they were dressed, what they talked about, and their general appearance and manner. After completing this assignment, she was able to stop focusing on job titles (i.e., "account executive at a large ad agency") and start focusing on the kinds of work she liked to do and the kind of people with whom she liked to do it.

Rebecca now holds the title "Director of Marketing" at a small, highly regarded design firm that specializes in package design for gourmet food products and wines. Like her work at the ad agency, her current job (1) involves daily contact with "creatives" as well as with business people, (2) gives her a great deal of exposure to clients as well as to co-workers, and (3) uses her talents as a persuasive writer and presenter. In addition, she is surrounded by people who dress fashionably, love exchanging gossipy tidbits about others in the industry, and like to talk about the best restaurants, movies, plays, and concerts in town—just like her cohorts at the ad agency.

Rebecca's experience is worth considering because she faced a dilemma many job seekers share these days. Demand for the work she had done was declining in the industry with which she was familiar, and the industry itself was (and still is) going through difficult times and consolidation. Advertising agencies, banks, insurance companies, government agencies, manufacturing companies and marketing concerns are all cutting back, and they are making many of their cuts within the ranks of midcareer managers and professionals. "Flattened pyramids" are being touted as the way of the future by all sorts of management gurus. Added to the toll taken by recessionary pressures, this infatuation with lean-and-mean management suggests that many people will not be able to find jobs comparable to the ones they lost. If you face a dilemma similar to Rebecca's—you feel the perfect job for you would essentially be the one you lost, but you realize a similar job may be almost impossible to find—you might want to begin to search for alternatives the way she did.

Make a chart that breaks the work day into half-hour intervals (for some people 15-minute intervals or hour intervals may be more appropriate) and recreate a typical day at your former job. Record what you would be doing, where you would be doing it, and with whom you would be interacting. Then describe the people with whom you would be having contact. Use the exercise to help you think in terms of desirable activities and cohorts instead of in terms of job titles.

MONEY MATTERS

So far you have been concerned with identifying what you want and breaking out of habitual ways of thinking about yourself that may prevent you from defining what you truly want and value. When the question of money enters the picture, however, you may feel that your values and desires must take second place to necessity. You have to pay the rent or pay off the mortgage; you have to send the kids through school, and within the next two years, you're going to need a new car. Like many Americans, you may have accumulated quite a substantial debt through credit cards and personal loans. Besides which, you don't want to give up skiing vacations or weekends at the beach.

After termination, you must grapple with two difficult questions of personal finance. First, how are you going to pay the bills until you find another job? Second, how much do you need to make in your next job to maintain an acceptable lifestyle?

Paradoxically, many people who have spent their professional lives dealing with budgets or with the financial affairs and accounting requirements of organizations have never tracked their personal expenses, formulated a household budget, or regularly checked their monthly bank statements. I suspect that credit cards and electronic banking contribute to many people's relaxed attitudes toward personal accounting; who cares about the balance in the checking account when you can always say "charge it" or get a cash advance from the automatic teller? If this is the way you have operated in the past, you will have to change your habits. Otherwise, your freedom to seek satisfying employment will be severely compromised.

Regardless of how you have managed your finances up to this point, you should sit down and take stock. Plan on being out of work for *at least* six months. You may find work sooner, but you may also take significantly longer to get settled into new employment. So, begin by listing your current sources of income, which may include severance pay, unemployment benefits (for which you should file as soon as possible, no matter how much you would like to avoid doing so), your spouse's income, payments from a former spouse, interest and dividend income, and so on. Next list potential interim sources of money—savings, gifts or loans from family members or friends, fees from consulting or part-time work, tax refunds, and sale of liquid assets.

You should not feel bad about asking others for financial aid. Easier said than done, of course, when you are accustomed to being financially independent. Look at your situation this way: you are asking others to invest in your future, not to give you a handout. Taking the time now to find work that is truly good for you, rather than feeling forced to take the first job you come across, will pay off in countless ways for many years to come. Remember, too, that the happier you are, the happier your family and loved ones will be: they will also benefit from your taking the time to find work that is right for you.

Having assessed your income situation, you should examine your expenses. Do not merely guesstimate—track your actual expenses as accurately as you can, using bank statements, receipts, credit card statements, and so on. Now you are ready for the big challenge—figuring out how to make your projected income cover your projected expenses. If you have ample severance benefits, some consulting or free-lance opportunities, and a spouse's income to help you through, you may have little difficulty weathering many months of unemployment. If you are not so fortunate, you may have to look for ways to lower your expenses.

Most of us spend a fair amount of money daily on inessentials such as movies, video rentals, cable TV, wine and liquor, dinners out, microwave meals, tobacco, magazines, records or tapes or CDs, clothes, and health club memberships. All make good candidates for cutbacks. In fact, you may now have a golden opportunity to ditch some of those expensive but unhealthy habits you have acquired over the years! One friend of mine realized after losing her job that with cigarettes costing over two dollars a pack, she was spending nearly $100 a month on her smoking habit. Smoke Enders, hypnosis, and acupuncture treatments had all failed to break her habit, but the prospect of saving $100 a month when her cash flow was low enabled her to smoke her last cigarette.

As you look for ways to economize, however, don't deprive yourself of all your former sources of pleasure. Getting out for a meal and a movie (or whatever you most like to do) is important during the stressful process of looking for a job. If you give up your health club membership, take up walking, jogging, calisthenics, or aerobic routines you can do at home. Now, more than ever, you need to treat yourself well, rewarding yourself for progress and persistence from time to time.

Bear in mind also that you will need to spend money to equip yourself for your job search. You should have some calling cards made up (calling cards are essentially business cards without an organizational affiliation), get yourself some good stationery, and buy or lease a phone-answering machine. If you don't have a typewriter or personal computer with a high-quality printer, you may want to buy or lease this kind of equipment, too. You will need to do a fair amount of photocopying and mailing, the expense of which can mount quickly. Finally, depending on the shape of your wardrobe, you may want to invest in one or two interviewing outfits. You do not need to be extravagant—you don't need the most expensive stationery available or the most advanced word-processing software on the market—but neither should you scrimp.

If you are tackling personal financial management for the first time, you might want to get more advice on how to keep records, cut costs, and make the most of your financial assets. Two recent books can give you more extensive guidance:

How to Avoid a Mid-Life Financial Crisis by Richard Eisenberg (Penguin Books, 1988).

How to Live Within Your Means and Still Finance Your Dreams by Robert Ortalda (Simon & Schuster, 1989).

One more word about personal finances during the job search: keep scrupulous records of all search-related expenses and save your receipts. Most are tax deductible. Keep a journal of these expenses and make daily en-

tries to record: transportation to and from interviews and other search-
related activities, such as meetings at your job club; phone calls; lunches
with contacts; postage; photocopying; stationery supplies; books about job
searching; and membership fees for professional organizations. If in
doubt about the deductibility of an expense, record it—you can subtract
it later if necessary.

Your review of your current financial situation should pave the way for
determining how much you need to make in your next position. Making
this determination is crucial but very difficult. Most of us have been
conditioned to equate money with freedom—we feel free when we are
free to buy anything we want—but *the more income you require, the less
freedom you have in making vocational choices.* All too often, real or
imagined financial requirements prevent people from making career
moves toward jobs more consistent with their values, talents, and desires.
Unfortunately, distinguishing between real and imagined needs is very
tricky, particularly in a society that measures success primarily in financial terms.

You alone can determine the price tag on your happiness, but as you
assess your situation in order to define an acceptable range of income,
consider the following accounts:

• Six months after Alex was promoted into a position where he earned
close to $100K a year, he was fired. Alex had no quarrel with the decision
because he agreed that his performance had been questionable and that
he had taken an extraordinary amount of sick leave without having any
major illnesses. He readily admitted that he had never liked the position
or the people with whom it brought him into contact and that most of his
sick days had resulted from being unable to face another day in the office.

He insisted, however, that he had to "make at least as much" in his
next job as he had made in his last and decided that to do so, he would
have to seek a similar position in a similar kind of organization. He got
one with little difficulty, largely because he was a likable fellow, a good
talker, and had made many contacts in his field. But within a year, he
was again out of a job—this time because he repeatedly showed up drunk
at meetings with clients.

• Kate was a fast-track MBA from Harvard who within five years of
graduation was earning $95K as vice president of marketing for a com-
pany that packaged and sold gourmet foods. Her true love, however, was
magazine publishing, which she had abandoned because she didn't feel

she could earn enough in the publishing industry. To prove her point, she often ran through a listing of her current expenses, which included:

$800 a month for psychotherapy, which she had been doing intensively for four and a half years.

$200 a month for massage and chiropractic adjustments, which she explained she needed because her back and neck muscles went into spasms when she was tense.

$200 a month for health club membership so she could relax in the steam room and sauna after work, without which she was unable to sleep.

$400 a month on marijuana because she needed something to "free up" her mind to "think creatively" when working under the pressure of deadlines.

$300 a month to garage her car, which she felt she needed in New York City so she could "get away quickly on weekends."

$200 a month to have her apartment cleaned, even though she was single and professed to actually enjoy housework, for which she simply didn't have time.

"Even though I'm making $95K, I still live from paycheck to paycheck," she notes with a sign of resignation.

• Maryann's company went into bankruptcy, and she was let go along with most of the other people in her division. She had enjoyed her former job as director of public relations, but she took a job selling insurance within six weeks of termination. She disliked her new job yet professed to be glad to have it because she "couldn't afford more than a couple of months of unemployment." When asked why, she explained that she had promised her son a car when he graduated from high school, and the car he wanted carried an $8,000 price tag. "Without a job, I could never have gotten a loan to buy it for him."

• Edward resigned from his position as a computer programmer for a large university and began doing similar work as a free-lancer for a variety of colleges and universities in the Boston area. When he left, he had been earning about $40K a year, but as a free-lancer, he was getting by on about half that amount. Despite his reduced income, he said he was happier than he had ever been before in his adult life because he was now able to devote two or three days a week to oil painting. He said his ability to get by on less demonstrated "the expense of having a 'real' job."

"Now I spend almost nothing on clothes because I don't have to dress in a suit and tie unless I'm meeting with clients. I no longer spend $75 a month just to get to and from my job, and I don't spend an additional $50 a month on magazines to read during the commute. You know, I must have spent over $100 a month on little crap like candy bars, coffee, donuts, and awful sandwiches from vending machines. Plus, now I almost never eat dinner out—when working full time, I always felt too tired to cook, but now I enjoy it. In fact, I get a kick out of buying inexpensive food at the grocery store and turning it into great meals."

These tales demonstrate the high cost, both emotionally and financially, of working in a job you dislike or that causes you to be tense, angry, and anxious most of the time. They also demonstrate the subjectivity involved in assessing financial needs. Did Maryann's son need to have an $8,000 car—or any car for that matter—and did she have to buy it for him? Did Kate need to earn $95K a year so she could afford to spend over $2,000 a month to recover from the ravages of her job? How badly did Alex need a $100 + K job that he would lose in less than a year?

As you explore your own financial needs, take time to sit down with your family or lover or spouse and discuss finances openly. If you decide that getting the job you want means taking a cut in pay, talk about what that will mean for those who depend on you financially: get them involved in discussing and solving the problems that may arise. Brainstorm with them (or with a close friend, if you are unattached) about ways to cut expenses and generate additional income. Above all, remember that vocational dissatisfaction is tremendously expensive and that it is just as costly for those you love as it is for you.

GATHERING INFORMATION

Discovering where you can get the work and generate the income you want is the next step in the quest for more satisfying employment. Like self-exploration, however, it is a step that is often short-changed. To many people, gathering information about employment opportunities means looking through the help-wanted sections of newspapers or professional publications. These are important sources of information, which you should certainly consult, but if they are the only sources of information you use, you will be missing many of the most attractive opportunities. In addition, you will not be doing a very effective job of preparing to promote yourself to potential employers.

Sources of Information

Help-wanted ads.   Experts estimate that between 50 and 80 percent of all employment opportunities never make their way into published notices. What's more, many of the openings that do get published are phantom opportunities. Organizations advertise openings for many reasons, only one of which is to actually fill positions. Some advertise openings to meet affirmative action requirements or organizational hiring policies when the position is already tagged for an insider. Some advertise as a means of gathering information about the labor market—to see who is out there looking for employment and how much they cost; in turn, this information is used to create a job description and establish a salary range consistent with the market, which is then used to fill positions internally.

Private placement firms.   Placement agencies and executive search firms (headhunters) also represent sources of information about job opportunities. Like help-wanted ads, however, their usefulness is limited. Remember: placement agencies and headhunters work for organizations seeking employees, not for individuals seeking employment. They serve primarily as screening and information-gathering mechanisms; ultimately, the hiring organization itself must make the final selection. In a sense, therefore, agencies and search firms can only say "no" to a job seeker; they can never say "yes" because they do not have hiring authority. You have little to lose, however, by using placement agencies or search firms—as long as you use them intelligently.

Using placement agencies and search firms intelligently means first and foremost not using them to the exclusion of other sources of information and not expecting them to generate interviews for you while you sit back waiting for the phone to ring. Once you have gotten your name and credentials registered with a firm, you need to follow up regularly, calling or dropping by fairly frequently to remind them of your existence and your value. Second, register with several. Third, select those with whom you register carefully. Make sure they handle a reasonable volume of positions like those you are seeking; otherwise you may find yourself being sent out to interview for jobs that bear little resemblance to what you have in mind—jobs for which you are well qualified, but in which you have no interest. Many placement and search firms get paid only when a position is filled by someone they have sent for an interview, so they have a strong incentive to send you out for any job that you *could* do, which is very different from sending you out for jobs that you want to do.

For help in locating placement and search firms, consult:

Career Guide Handbook—Membership Directory. This annual publication is prepared by the National Association of Personnel Consultants and lists personnel agencies throughout the United States. It is widely available in libraries.

Directory of Executive Recruiters. Put together by *Consultants News* and published annually, this directory lists firms alphabetically and indicates each firm's area of specialization. Also widely available in libraries.

State employment agencies. There's no harm in consulting the postings in your local office. Many offices also provide free workshops in job-search skills. For the most part, however, their postings tend to be for lower-level positions and to be heavily concentrated in the public sector.

Job banks. Most states and some private firms now maintain computerized job banks. In theory, they keep on file the names and credentials of people seeking jobs and match them with job openings sent to them by organizations (including government agencies) seeking to fill positions. Getting yourself into such systems can't hurt, although some of the private ones charge for keeping your file active. However, I have never known personally anyone who got a job this way. I have, on the other hand, heard some amusing (in retrospect, at least) stories of people receiving rejection letters from jobs for which they didn't even know they were being considered!

Your two major sources of information about employment possibilities should be LIBRARIES and NETWORKING, and these sources should be used to complement one another.

Libraries

Any reasonably well-stocked library will contain a veritable wealth of information on industries, companies, positions, and decision makers within organizations. Many libraries have special collections designed specifically to help people who are looking for jobs, as well as special business collections. In addition, libraries have librarians—people trained to help you locate the information you need and to help you identify what kind of information you need to answer particular questions. Some libraries even offer computer programs to help you through the process of vocational self-exploration. If your local library is too small to provide the reference materials you need, check out the libraries at nearby colleges and universities and ask your local librarians for the addresses of larger libraries in the region that can provide the information you seek. Local libraries are usually parts of larger countywide and statewide library systems.

A word of caution before we explore in greater depth how to use library research in your job search: *Do the research yourself.* Don't hire someone else to do it or fall for the line some outplacement firms push, which is that you will be too busy doing more important things during your job search to waste time in a library. Outplacement firms often provide research services as part of their package, and they are eager to have you use these services, for which, of course, you or your former employer will have to pay. Many outplacement counselors, therefore, advise clients to let trained, professional researchers gather information, insisting that clients do not have the necessary skills and should not be bothered with developing them. If you buy this line, you will lose out on most of the benefits library research has to offer.

I cannot stress too strongly the wisdom of viewing a job search as a creative activity. Creative activities require immersion. Before you can solve a problem creatively, you must immerse yourself in it and in information about it. Library research immerses you in information about potential employers and employment opportunities. When you use a professional researcher, he or she gets the benefits of immersion, not you. Also, a researcher's job is to exclude irrelevant information as well as to find relevant information. A good researcher can determine what information is and is not relevant to answering a specific question but cannot determine what information is or is not relevant to *you.* Some of the most helpful information you will find in the course of your research will be "irrelevant" information you come upon by accident as you search for "relevant" information.

By doing the research yourself, you will be developing skills and gaining knowledge that will be useful in your next job and in almost every aspect of your life for the rest of your days. How many times have you

ead the phrase, "this is the information age"? If you don't know
nd how to find information, you are a severely handicapped
dritte₁ n the information age. On the other hand, if you learn how to
find information about organizations and the people in them, you will
have learned something useful in making investments, marketing products or services, selecting schools for your children or yourself, deciding
what insurance to buy or what bank to use, figuring out which car to
purchase, finding a good nursing home for an aging parent, or determining whether the company that wants to build a plant near your neighbor-
hood has a decent record concerning environmental pollution.

Sleuthing is perhaps the best way of thinking about the research you
will be conducting in your job search. Like the many sleuths on TV, in
movies, and in books, you will be successful to the extent that you are
both persistent and imaginative in seeking information. The sources of
printed information presented in the bibliography at the end of this chapter represent only the tip of a very vast iceberg, but if you start with them
and use them well, you will soon find yourself discovering the huge body
of information below the surface.

Anyone conducting a systematic job search will at some point need to
get information on *positions and job titles, salaries, industries,* and *companies*; most will also want to get information about *individual people.* All
these kinds of information should be sought both from libraries and informational interviewing.

Positions and job titles. If you are not sure what kinds of positions correspond most closely to your ideal job description, you will want
to consult a dictionary or directory of job titles. At the end of the chapter,
you will find a list of the most comprehensive standard references. If you
are contemplating a career change, you will probably want to consult *The
Encyclopedia of Second Careers,* which can help you match your experience, skills, and education with positions different from the ones you
have pursued in the past. Unlike most other general references on job
titles, this one is geared not to first-time job seekers but to people who
want to apply previous experiences to new occupations.

Salaries. Information about salary ranges for different positions
and in different geographical areas is important at two points in your job
search. In the initial stages of your search, you will want to find out
whether the kind of work that most interests you pays what you want or

need to earn. At the end of your search, with one or more offers in hand, you will need up-to-date information about salaries in your field in order to negotiate effectively the terms of employment. Also, at almost any point in the selection process, you may be asked about your salary requirements and you will want to be able to respond with a realistic range.

Information about industries and companies.   Information on industries and companies helps you in two very important ways during your job search. First, it helps you narrow your search to a relatively small number of organizations that: (1) employ people to do the kind of work you would like to do, (2) currently need people who do what you want to do, and (3) have policies and philosophies consistent with your values and preferences. Having narrowed your search, you can mount a concerted campaign to get offers from your target organizations. Without this kind of targeting, much of your marketing effort will be wasted on organizations that do not offer what you want or that do not want what you offer. Many marketing mavens say the days of mass marketing are numbered. In today's markets, targeted campaigns directed at carefully defined audiences get the best results. Take your cues from the marketing professionals.

Second, information on industries and companies enables you to identify the problems and opportunities your targeted organizations face. Then you can present yourself as someone able to help solve these problems and exploit these opportunities, rather than as someone merely qualified to fill a position. If you are merely qualified, or even well qualified to fill a position, you will be almost indistinguishable from dozens— perhaps hundreds—of other similarly qualified candidates. But if you take the time to do your homework and do it well, you will stand out from the crowd. Believe me: most of the people who read this book or who read other books making similar recommendations or who get similar advice from placement and outplacement counselors will disregard it. They will apply for positions in organizations about which they know little more than the organization's name and address. Those folks will make it easy for you to stand out.

You should always do some homework before going on informational interviews as well as before going on selection interviews. Since the notion of networking has become popular, more and more people are hitting the networking trail, which means more and more people in organizations are being hit up more and more often for informational interviews. Almost nothing annoys busy people more than being asked for information that could have been gotten from a quick skimming of the annual report or from the most casual review of periodical literature or even from the yellow pages.

Throughout your search, you should stay abreast of current business developments at both the national and local level. Read the business sections of one or more nationally available newspapers such as *The Wall Street Journal* and *The New York Times* at least two or three times a week and regularly look through local newspapers from the geographical areas in which you are searching. Libraries generally subscribe to several newspapers, so you need not spend a fortune to keep yourself up-to-date.

If you have difficulty finding information on a specific company, various references can at least give you a better feel for the industry group to which it belongs. In addition, industry overviews are very helpful in identifying the kinds of opportunities and challenges companies in a particular industry face or can expect to face in the future. From overviews, you can determine whether an industry is growing or declining, dominated by a few large companies or characterized by numerous smaller companies, facing increased foreign competition, heavily or lightly regulated, and so on.

Information on individuals.   Finding out about individual people allows you to send your résumé and cover letters directly to appropriate individuals in appropriate areas of organizations. Information on particular people can also help you prepare for interviews and can give you a better sense of an organization's character.

Even if you are sending your résumé to the people in personnel or human resources, it is a good idea to have the name of a particular person to whom to address it. More important, if you send materials to the human resources department, you should also send them to people in the functional areas, departments, or divisions where you want to work, and you should have the names of one or more specific people to whom to address them.

The role, strength, and structure of human resources and personnel departments vary widely from one organization to the next. In some, people from human resources play an important role in selecting employees for positions at all levels and are involved in all phases of the selection process. In others, they serve only as screening mechanisms or are truly involved in the selection process only for lower-level positions.

Some organizations have highly centralized human resources departments; others integrate human resources experts into each functional area, department, and division so that they can work closely with line personnel. In some organizations, sending your résumé to the human resources department is equivalent to sending it into a black hole; in others it is the best way to get your foot in the door. The moral is this: *you have not really explored the possibilities in an organization if you send your résumé only to the main personnel department, so you need ways to identify people in other areas of organizations with whom to discuss employment opportunities.*

Whatever your source of a name and information on an individual, take the time to phone the organization with which he or she is affiliated before mailing anything. Personnel turn over rapidly in organizations these days, and you should make sure the person still works there and confirm the title, address, and phone number you have uncovered in your sleuthing.

Networking

Networking and library research, as noted earlier, go hand in hand and should be pursued simultaneously. Library research will yield ideas, companies, and people you will want to explore further through informational interviewing; likewise, talking with people will generate ideas and possibilities you will want to explore further through printed sources and/ or electronic data bases.

Your first networking job is to let just about everyone you can think of know that you are looking for work. For people who have recently been terminated, this is often a daunting task. But the longer you put if off, the harder it will become. If necessary, keep reminding yourself that very, very, *very* few successful people have made it through life without having lost jobs involuntarily. Most, in fact, have plenty of rejection stories to tell, from being rejected by schools to being ejected from jobs. As one retired CEO of a large manufacturing company said to me during a recent interview, "Anyone who has never been fired has probably never had the guts to take any risks and probably should have been fired many times over."

In your networking, you will doubtless run into people who will implicitly or explicitly blame you for being out of work. They'll suggest variously that you were wrong to take that job to begin with or that if you had played your cards right, you would still have it or that you should have seen the handwriting on the wall long ago and left before being shown the door. Often these people will be people close to you, like parents, in-laws, siblings, spouses, or lovers, which will make their blaming all the more difficult to bear. Take a deep breath, look them in the eye, and say calmly, "Well, unfortunately, that's water over the dam at this point, and I'd like your help in getting on with my life. Here's what you could do for me. . . ."

Try to avoid arguing with them. Doing so will probably just make you feel angrier and stand in the way of your getting the real help they may be able to offer. Instead of arguing, try to engage them in the problem-solving process of finding new employment. Ask them to help you think of people with whom you might talk about jobs. Share with them some of the options you are considering and invite them to brainstorm with you about how to investigate them. Ask them about their own experiences of losing or changing jobs and get them to describe some of the search techniques they found helpful. Encourage them to share their experiences and to provide concrete information or resources that may be useful to you.

Begin your networking close to home, and tackle the task systematically. Set up a network worksheet as shown in Figure 6. Then sit down and work on it until you have filled in absolutely as many names as you can. Under the heading "professional helpers" include people like your accountant, physician, dentist, therapist, financial adviser, minister or rabbi, and so on. Next, decide for each whether to make your initial contact by phone or in writing.

There are no hard and fast rules for determining which approach is best in any given case; what is most appropriate depends on the closeness of your current relationship, your past patterns of communication, what sort of help you are seeking, and your personal preferences concerning phoning *versus* writing. In general, however, plan to follow up your initial contact with the other mode of communication; that is, if you make your first contact by phone, follow up with a note or letter, and if you write first, follow up with a phone call.

Never plan to simply sit and wait for contacts to get back to you again after your initial communication, no matter what form that communication takes. One of the keys to successful networking is to keep active those portions of the net you have already jiggled while continuing to activate new portions. Whenever you think "contact" (whether it be for the first or

FIGURE 6
Network Worksheet

I. Undergraduate and graduate schools; corporate training; and development programs

Fellow Students

1._____ 4._____ 7._____

2._____ 5._____ 8._____

3._____ 6._____ 9._____

Faculty and Administration

1._____ 3._____ 5._____

2._____ 4._____ 6._____

II. Friends and neighbors

1._____ 4._____ 7._____

2._____ 5._____ 8._____

3._____ 6._____ 9._____

III. Business associates

1._____ 4._____ 7._____

2._____ 5._____ 8._____

3._____ 6._____ 9._____

IV. Professional helpers

1._____ 3._____ 5._____

2._____ 4._____ 6._____

V. Relatives

1._____ 3._____ 5._____

2._____ 4._____ 6._____

the fifth time) think "follow up." Be professional about following up even with relatives and friends—your courtesy will be appreciated by all those who aid you in your quest.

Staying connected takes creativity as well as good record keeping and thoughtfulness. You don't want to seem like a pest, so you will sometimes have to be inventive in discovering occasions for correspondence and conversation. Thank-you notes are an obvious means of following up,

but there are others as well. As you conduct your library research, you
will come across articles, news items, and books related to topics you have
discussed in interviews, and you can use them as opportunities to get back
to your contacts. Photocopy items of interest and send them along with a
calling card and a brief note reminding your contact of your discussion.
For example:

Dear Jim,

When we met last month to talk about job opportunities at your firm, you
mentioned your interest in new ventures in the bio-engineering field. As I
read the attached article, your comments came to mind, and I thought you
might find Zertex, Inc.'s story as fascinating as I did.

Sincerely (or "Warmly" or "Cordially"),

The degree of formality in such notes should depend on your relationship to the receiver, the warmth of your last communication, your personal style, and the personal style of the person to whom they are ad-
dressed. They need not be typed as long as you have legible handwriting.
Whether you push the receiver for further action in such notes is a tricky
judgment call. You might, for example, add a paragraph saying something like:

The more I learn about venture capital firms, the more eager I become to
work for ABC, Inc. If any opportunities open up, please let me know.

You can also follow up with notes or letters updating contacts on the
progress of your search. If your contact gave you names of additional
people with whom to get in touch, write or call after talking with them.
Likewise, if your situation changes—for example, if you decide to take
some courses or broaden your search to other geographical areas—let
previous contacts know. Beware, however, of becoming too casual or
unbusinesslike with contacts. It is not appropriate in most cases to write
notes (or make phone calls) that say something on the order of:

Hi!
It's been a couple of months since we got together, and I just thought I'd drop
a line to see how you're doing. Let me hear from you.

Indirection is the major flaw in the above sample. The note serves no
purpose and suggests that you wrote (or called) mainly because you happened to have nothing better to do for the moment.

FIGURE 7
Contact Cards

NAME   PHONE NUMBER
TITLE
ORGANIZATION
ADDRESS + ZIP

Referred by:
Name of assistant or secretary:

Date of initial contact—followed by a brief description that includes method of
  contact, info. exchanged, and follow up indicated.

Date of next contact—summarize as indicated above.

Date—summary

Date—summary

Ms. Jane Doe   (201) 875-4920
VP/Director of Marketing
ABC, INC.
246 W. Front St.
Claymon, N.J.

ref by: Tom Claxton

9/18 called; asked for resume; sent w/cover letter: 9/19

9/27 follow-up call to make appt. On vacation. Left
     message & will call back next wk.

10/3 returned call; apt made for 10/10 at 10:30 AM

10/9 called to confirm appt.
                                        (see back)

EXAMPLE

Make a contract with yourself establishing a minimum number of networking calls and letters for each day or each week. Depending on how stressful or enjoyable you find networking, you may want to set yourself a minimum of 2 a day or 10 a day. As your search progresses, you may want to modify your minimum, but require yourself to stick to the one you've set until you deliberately decide on a different one.

To keep track of your contacts and follow ups, get a pack of 4" × 6" or 5" × 7" index cards (3" × 5" cards are too small for this purpose), a box to keep them in, and a set of alphabetical dividers. Fill out a card as illustrated in Figure 7 for each contact. You should cross-reference your file according to organizational affiliation: include a card for each organization at which you have established one or more contacts. On it, record the names of all the individual contacts for whom you have separate cards elsewhere in your file. Be scrupulous about annotating cards each time you get in touch with someone. Don't trust your memory—if you're doing a good job of networking, you will not have the memory capacity to recall the dates and details of all your phone calls and correspondence.

Another key to successful networking is to continually build your network. Every time you establish contact with someone new, ask him or her for the names of at least two or three other people with whom you might get in touch. At first you might feel awkward about making this request, but it will soon become a matter of habit. Simply ask, "Can you think of some other people I might talk to about _____?" (getting jobs in financial management, working at ABC, starting my own business, going back to school in midcareer, moving from academia into private industry, going from corporate training into public-school teaching, launching a consulting practice, buying a franchise. . .). When you get names, be sure to write them down, get the right spelling, and establish the correct pronunciation. Then ask whether you may use the provider's name in your self-introduction. "Would you mind," you might ask, "my saying that you suggested I call?"

IT'S TIME TO REDEFINE

One purpose of your information gathering is to refine and add realism to your sense of the kind of work you want and the kind of organization you want to work for. As you collect information through library work and networking, you should periodically review your ideal job description and revise it to reflect your growing knowledge and your increasing commitment to a narrowing range of possibilities. If you don't feel that your commitment is growing or your range narrowing, review and revision can help you achieve these goals.

At the end of every week, take out your latest perfect job description, reread it, and make notes in the margins. Use the exercise to sum up your week's work. Every few weeks, do a full rewrite of the description, integrating the notes you have accumulated. In this process of continual review and revision, you will be transforming your ideal into a more concrete, achievable objective.

Your growing knowledge of both yourself and the current world of work should also enable you to identify obstacles that may stand in the way of reaching your employment objective. You may discover that to get the kind of position you want, you need a stronger background in marketing or finance or human resources or journalism. Or you may learn that in most companies in the industry most appealing to you, almost everyone above a certain level in the hierarchy has an M.B.A. Or you may decide that to continue moving upward in your previous field, you will simply have to learn more about computerized data bases and spreadsheets. Or you may realize that you feel uncomfortable in interviews and that you need to enhance your communication skills both to get a new job and to do well in it. Perhaps as you confront your emotional responses to the trauma of termination and the stress of job seeking, you realize that psychological problems stand in the way of your being productive at work and happy at home.

Identifying potential obstacles to reaching an objective and figuring out ways to overcome them is the very essence of creative problem solving. You need to perform this crucial step as thoroughly, honestly, and realistically as you can. Sit down with a blank sheet of paper and your ideal job description/employment objective. Read the description carefully, title the blank sheet "Potential Obstacles," and list any and all that come to mind. In addition to the sorts identified in the previous paragraph, consider ones like:

- Not having enough time for the demanding job you want in light of current family responsibilities.
- Not having enough money to go to school for additional training.
- Not being able to afford to travel to distant cities where you would like to interview for jobs.
- Problems with alcohol or drugs.

- Feeling too depressed to do well in interviews.
- Not knowing how to get money to start a business of your own.

Next, for each obstacle, list several possible ways to overcome or get around it. This is a good time to enlist the aid of friends, lovers, and family members. In addition to supplementing your imagination, they will probably be among your chief resources for overcoming problems. The sooner you get them involved in the problem-solving process, the more committed they will be to the solutions you decide to pursue. Be open to all sorts of possibilities at this point; you can return to them later for critical assessment.

Through the process of identifying obstacles and finding ways around them, you will be developing a set of intermediate objectives. You will be breaking down your journey to your employment objective into manageable steps. Let's look at an example to see how this works.

Suppose your background is in human resources management, and you have worked for several years at a large firm in the financial services industry. Your self-exploration and information gathering have led you to conclude that you want to move into general management in the same industry, but you have identified your relative lack of financial knowledge as one obstacle and prejudice against "human resources types" within the industry as another. Now you have in a sense defined a new, intermediate objective: acquiring knowledge and credibility in the area of finance. Your next step would be to identify ways to reach this new objective. Taking courses might be one; reading everything in sight about finance and the financial services industry might be another; doing financial management or analysis work on a part-time or volunteer basis for a community group might be a third.

As you assess these options, you may identify additional potential obstacles. Courses are expensive, and you never liked being a student anyway. Teaching yourself may seem more appealing, but then you face the problem of convincing potential employers that you have the knowledge you claim. You could perhaps get around this obstacle by proving your acumen through voluntary work or by managing a portfolio of securities for your family, but proving yourself through these activities would require you to establish a track record, before which you would have to educate yourself in finance—a very time-consuming process that would actually be quite expensive considering the time lost to paid employment. So, you conclude taking courses would be the best option. Now you have defined a new objective: to figure out where such courses are offered, which you should take, and how to raise the money for them.

Notice that defining objectives, identifying obstacles, and figuring out how to get around the obstacles is a continuous process. As you engage in this process, you continually generate new, intermediate objectives, thus reducing what may at first seem like a huge barrier to smaller and smaller pieces. Eventually you will reach a point where you can pick up the pieces and cast them aside one at a time.

INVESTING IN YOUR DEVELOPMENT

As you identify obstacles and consider ways of overcoming them, you may conclude—as in the example above—that the best way around an obstacle involves getting some form of expert help. This help may take the form of schooling, coaching, counseling, psychotherapy, reading, or some combination of these options. Seeking expert help, however, often requires facing a new set of challenges: finding money for it and finding truly helpful experts to provide it.

Regarding money, many out-of-work people face both financial and psychological problems. You may be reluctant to spend more money at a time when you are earning less and feel uncertain about your future prospects. In the long run, however, you may save a great deal of money by investing in yourself now. It makes more sense to liquidate some assets and borrow money than to prolong your job search by deciding, for example, not to get coaching on your interviewing technique. If you brush up on interviewing the hard way—by going through numerous unsuccessful interviews and learning from experience (which, by the way, often simply does not happen in the absence of feedback, no matter how many interviews you endure)—you may spend an extra month or two unemployed. Even at a modest salary level that nets you $1,500 to $2,000 a month in take-home pay, you may be forfeiting several thousand dollars in the near future to avoid spending a hundred dollars now.

If you carefully define the kind of help you need and have a clear sense of how it relates to your employment objective, you will probably find that you can figure out affordable ways to get it or ways to raise money to afford it. Your conviction will inspire the confidence of family and friends, which will make them more willing to lend you money, in part because they will be persuaded of your ability to pay them back.

The good news and the bad news about selecting appropriate sources of expert help is that there are lots of so-called experts out there and lots of different approaches to providing help and lots of different notions about what is truly helpful. To help you find your way through the maze, the following section briefly describes the kinds of help you might want to consider during your job search.

SOURCES OF EXPERT HELP DURING VOCATIONAL TRANSITION

Outplacement Services

Outplacement counseling is a relatively new profession, and the folks who provide it come from a wide variety of backgrounds. The term *outplacement counselor* is not a protected professional title, which means there are no laws limiting its use—anyone can call her- or himself an outplacement counselor. In some respects, the absence of licensing or certification requirements in this field is fortunate. It has allowed the field to attract an eclectic group of individuals, many of whom bring to their work a wonderful mix of knowledge and experience.

Some counselors are former executives with a flair for coaching and a strong background in psychology. Some are graduates of programs in clinical or counseling psychology with strong backgrounds in the psychology of vocational choice and experience working in organizations. Some have gotten their training on the job by working for large outplacement firms; many are seasoned professionals from human resources departments of large organizations.

Almost all counselors offer help with devising a search strategy, revising résumés, creating cover letters, and enhancing interview skills. Most also provide some rudimentary help in self-assessment and making vocational choices—figuring out employment objectives. Such help may take the form of vocational testing and/or individual sessions during which you explore the reasons for your termination, your assets, and your preferences concerning type, size, and location of organization; income; career path; and working conditions. Many also offer research services, which as you know, I recommend refusing.

When organizations provide outplacement services to terminated employees, the level of service can vary widely, depending on your former position in the hierarchy. Top executives will get office space, secretarial support, access to fax machines, computers, high-quality printers, and other office equipment, and much individual attention from counselors. Middle managers and professionals may be offered workshops on job-search skills and a few private counseling sessions. Lower-level managers and office workers may be offered only workshops or nothing at all.

When you are terminated, it pays to ask what might be available for you and to find out what the biggest wheels get. You might as well ask for the complete package—you have nothing to lose. You might also try to get an allowance for expert help that you can spend as you see fit as long as you spend it on something reasonably related to making your vocational transition.

If you are looking for outplacement services on your own, ask for a consultation before making a choice. When approaching firms, rather than individual counselors, ask to meet with whomever will actually supply your counseling. Some smaller firms contract out much of their work, and meeting with the head of the firm will tell you little about the person with whom you will be working primarily. Outplacement firms often supply a team of professionals; each member works with you on a different aspect of your search. This approach is excellent; it works best, I believe, when the client has a co-ordinating or primary counselor with whom to work closely throughout the process. This person should be a member of the team, serving as your project manager within it, as well as being your primary counselor outside it.

Ask prospective counselors to show you their résumés or professional biographies, and beware of anyone who cannot or will not provide a copy: at a minimum, a person offering help with an employment search should have an up-to-date version of his or her own credentials to share with clients. Look for evidence of (1) some formal training in counseling psychology, (2) work within organizations other than outplacement firms or in-house outplacement departments, and (3) substantial experience helping people at your level find jobs.

Career Counseling

Outplacement firms supply career counseling, but career counselors do not necessarily supply outplacement services. Career or vocational counseling focuses on formulating a vocational objective, rather than on implementing it. Individual counselors vary widely in terms of their ability to help you through the process of achieving your objective.

Many career counselors rely heavily on standardized testing instruments, which are essentially surveys. Your responses to questions are statistically compared with the results of other test takers. The validity of the results depends on how many people have already taken the survey, how similar you are to previous test takers, how well the questions have been formulated, and how intelligently the results are interpreted. Many vocational tests essentially tell you how similar you are to others currently in the field you are pursuing. A good counselor will be good at selecting testing instruments appropriate to you, interpreting the results *with* you (not *to* you), and helping you use the results to make vocational choices.

Testing can be helpful, but should not replace more open-ended forms of self-exploration. Take tests as part of your self-exploration, not as all of it. Many career counselors can help you with both standardized tests and more open-ended exercises. Quite a few have backgrounds in psychological counseling and can be emotionally supportive to you during your search; most, however, are not trained in communications skills and coaching, thus they cannot help you much with documenting your achievements or handling interviews. Two or three visits to a career counselor with testing expertise can be a helpful supplement to other sources of counseling expertise during your search. You can expect to pay from $25 to $95 an hour for their time.

Some of the best experts can be found at colleges or universities near you. Many schools train people to become vocational counselors, and the folks doing the training are usually experienced counselors who also work with individuals. The training programs themselves sometimes offer low-cost testing opportunities. Look in graduate schools of education as well as in graduate schools of psychology.

Communications Coaching

Communications coaching is an up-and-coming field (I will confess to prejudice) attracting professionals from a variety of backgrounds, often in teaching writing or performance. They can help you with and through the composition and revision of résumés, cover letters, proposals, sales letters, and any other documents you may find useful in your transition to new employment. Many can also coach you for interviews both of the informational and employment varieties.

The best sources of coaches are graduate professional schools—consult the one from which you graduated or one in your chosen field. Call and ask for the "communications program" or "management communications department" or the "communications skills training program" (there is no uniform terminology). Also consult placement departments. Someone in one or more of these areas should be able to refer you to a seasoned coach. Ask for someone with experience helping people who are looking for jobs at your level.

Hourly rates vary tremendously. Coaches to the "stars" may command $1,000 or more an hour. But most communications coaches charge more reasonably. Sessions with video start at about $75 an hour and may reach several hundreds an hour for on-site locations (i.e., when the coach travels to you). Writing expertise ranges from $45 to $120 an hour. Expect to pay more when your coach comes to you and to pay for editing time in addition to coaching sessions.

Psychotherapy

The array of approaches and terminology is bewildering—and somewhat deceptive. All good therapists achieve similar results and use similar techniques. Studies of outcomes across a wide variety of therapies suggest that the specific background of a therapist—whether he or she is an M.D. or an M.S.W., a psychoanalyst, existential psychoanalyst, or family therapist—bears little correlation with outcome. Neither the amount and kind of training nor theoretical orientation seem to matter much to the success of a therapeutic relationship. What does seem to matter are:

- How much you and your therapist like one another.
- How well you communicate with each other.
- How alike you are in terms of socioeconomic and educational background, intelligence, and relationship experience.
- How experienced your therapist is in providing therapy.

But one of the most complex questions about psychotherapy is what it should accomplish. Should it make you happy? Should it make you free? Should it make you behave? Good psychotherapy will accomplish what you want it to. What you truly and perhaps unconsciously want, psychotherapy should help you locate and in some sense realize. It will do so through insight, emotional support, and help in solving problems within relationships.

During a job search, problems in relationships sometimes surface dramatically. The stress of vocational transition puts a strain on personal relationships and may literally ruin your love life—being with those you love and doing what you love. Psychotherapy can, therefore, be very helpful during your career changes.

Therapy should also make you *feel* better. To do so, some forms of therapy use drugs primarily, some use talking techniques exclusively, and many combine them. If you feel you suffer from chronic depression, not just circumstantial depression caused by external events, you may want to try a combination of drug therapy and talking therapy. Ask prospective therapists how they feel about the use of drugs to relieve chronic anxiety, depression, or obsession. Many therapists do not, themselves, prescribe but will be able to help you decide whether drug therapy might be helpful for you and put you in touch with a specialist to evaluate your needs and prescribe for you.

Individual therapy can be very expensive, and prices range widely, depending on the credentials of your therapist. Bear in mind as you make your selection that the factors most highly correlated with success in psychotherapy are the ones listed earlier, not the educational background or theoretical orientation of your therapist. Group therapy can be a good supplement to or substitute for individual psychotherapy. It offers the advantages of being less expensive and exposing you to several other people, which can do wonders for psychic health and energy.

Reading (Bibliotherapy)

Reading is good for you, especially during a vocational transition. It can contribute to all of the forms of expert help described in this chapter. Check the psychology, self-help, career, and business collections in the libraries and bookstores you come across in your travels. Printed materials are expensive these days, so remember that you can get many of the things you want through your local library. If you don't see it, ask. Check magazines, periodicals, and other collections of nonbook information sources.

You might also want to explore some of the recent fictional and non-fictional portrayals of business relationships in the United States. Particularly fascinating and possibly helpful are portryals of job loss in contemporary fiction. Many recent novels feature characters who lose jobs as a result of mergers, restructurings, and the corporate political games that are played most fiercely during times of scarcity, uncertainty, and change. Although most of these books are not of great, enduring literary value, they hold a mirror up to the internal workings of modern organizations and reflect the psychological and emotional tolls associated with professional managerial positions. To get a feel for the range of organizational fiction our society is generating, check out:

Hocus Pocus, by Kurt Vonnegut.
Tender Offers, by Peter Engel.
Having It All, by Reva Korda.

Almost everyone I talk to wants to read more and has a list of at least a dozen books—ranging from classics to best-sellers—that they've been meaning to read for months or years. When you are between jobs, you have the time to make a dent in your reading debt.

Formal Education

Going back to school is the first thing some people think of between jobs; for others, it is an option of last resort. But continuing education is a condition of survival in a world of rapid change, whether you educate yourself, go to school, or seek the other kinds of expertise described throughout this section.

As you evaluate formal programs of education, look for schools that provide plenty of opportunities to learn through means other than attending lectures, reading textbooks, and taking tests. Most adults do best in educational settings that stress applying knowledge to real problems in realistic contexts, which is sometimes termed "clinical" training. Look for a mix of experienced clinicians and academics on the faculty. Look into the opportunities a school provides for self-directed study projects and for work in small groups of peers. If you are seeking graduate management education, above all look for programs with strong course offerings in professional communication—interviewing, preparing a variety of documents, negotiating, communicating in groups, speaking, and nonverbal communication. Every manager and professional in every field and at every level needs sophisticated communication skills to do a good job.

Finally, consider what a school offers in terms of resources outside the classroom. Libraries, placement services, counseling services, computer facilities, student organizations, and strong alumnae organizations can all contribute as much—or more—to your educational experience as what goes on in classes. Bookstores and libraries generally gather a number of guides to schools of all sorts and are a good place to start looking into programs. Don't neglect, however, other important information sources, particularly on-site visits and informational interviews with graduates.

INFORMATION SOURCES FOR JOB SEEKERS

Job Titles

If you need to determine the job titles or positions that correspond to the kinds of work you want to do and the skills you offer, consult:

Dictionary of Occupational Titles (DOT). Published by the U.S. Government Printing Office, this catalog lists approximately 13,000 occupations and is widely available in libraries.

Selected Characteristics of Occupations Defined in the Dictionary of Occupational Titles. Prepared by the Department of Labor, Employment and Training Administration and published by the U.S. Government Printing Office, this reference supplies more detailed information than the *DOT* on a variety of occupations.

Occupational Outlook Handbook. A volume revised biennially that covers occupations in 35 major industries. It is put together by the Bureau of Labor Statistics and published by the U.S. Government Printing Office.

Occupational Outlook Handbook for College Graduates. Similar to the above volume, but more limited.

The Encyclopedia of Second Careers, by Gene R Hawes (New York: Facts-on-File, 1984) is especially helpful if you are switching careers because opportunities look slim along your former career path.

There are also many books you can consult if you want more specific information on particular kinds of jobs and careers. For example:

Offbeat Careers: The Directory of Unusual Work, by Al Sacharov (Berkeley, Calif.: Ten Speed Press, 1988).

Alternative Careers for Teachers, by Marna Beard and Michael McGahey (New York: Arco Publishing, 1985).

The Consultant's Calling: Bringing who you are to what you do, by Geoffrey Bellman. (San Francisco: Jossey-Bass, 1990).

Job Creation in America by David Birch (New York: The Free Press, 1987). A good book for those who want to explore job opportunities in small companies, where most jobs are being created these days.

The Career Directory Series (Career Press, 1987). Each volume gives an overview of a field within the broad category of communications, provides sample job descriptions, and lists the names of trade organizations and publications. Individual titles in the series include:

Advertising Career Directory
Book Publishing Career Directory

Magazine Career Directory
Marketing and Sales Career Directory
Newspaper Career Directory
Public Relations Career Directory

The above list of more specialized books on particular kinds of work is far from complete. It is meant only to give you a feel for the range of materials available. There are also books specifically on careers and jobs in banks, insurance companies, government agencies, manufacturing companies, hospitals, and just about any other kind of organization you can name. There are also books organized around specific fields of knowledge, such as biology, finance, marketing, music, and so on. As you begin to narrow your sense of what you are looking for, consult your librarian for help. Also check large bookstores with varied collections, in which you will find a section on "Careers" or "Job Hunting" or "Business" (or all three). In these sections, you can find the latest publications in your area of interest, which may not make their way to your library for quite a while.

Salaries

The *Occupational Outlook Handbook* (see above for complete citation) gives basic salary information for each of the positions it lists and is a useful starting point. It is most helpful, however, in reference to entry-level positions. Other sources of salary overviews generally available at libraries are:

American Almanac of Jobs & Salaries by John W. Wright (New York: Avon, 1990).

National Survey of Professional, Administrative, Technical, and Clerical Pay issued annually by the U.S. Bureau of Labor Statistics. (You can get your own copy of the *National Survey* for about $5 directly from the Bureau.)

As you begin to define your employment objective more precisely and narrow your search, however, you should get more detailed information. You will probably want to know, for example, how quickly salaries in the field tend to rise; whether bonuses are generally given—and if so, on what basis and how large; how much variation in salary you might expect from one region to another; and whether other perks, such as company cars, routinely constitute a portion of the total compensation package. Professional associations and trade journals are generally good sources of more detailed compensation information. To get the names, addresses, and brief descriptions of the associations relevant to your interests, consult:

The Encyclopedia of Associations, edited by Denise Akey. (Detroit: Gale Research Company). Volume 1 contains a national listing of organizations; Volume 2 indexes organizations by geographical area and provides names and addresses of officers and directors of each. You can find this reference in almost any library, and it is revised frequently.

Professional and trade associations often publish journals, and many devote an issue each year to salary surveys. You can call the headquarters of associations to determine whether they collect and publish information on salaries and, if so, how you can get it.

One of the easiest ways to get detailed information on salaries and other forms of compensation tailored to your particular situation is through the:

Productivity Improvement Network (PIN)
Suite 6H, 10 Waterside Plaza
New York, NY 10010
(212) 685-3454.

PIN maintains a computer bank of salary information, which is used to create customized "Pay Range Reports." After you provide PIN with basic information about you and the positions on which you are seeking information, they will send you printouts from their data base that include salary ranges, typical job responsibilities, factors that usually affect compensation, typical perks, and the usual career paths for specific kinds of jobs. The fee for each "Pay Range Report" is $25, but PIN will send you a sample report for free if you want to get a better idea of what one contains before spending any money.

The fastest way to get information from PIN is by mailing them a brief letter explaining that you want a "Pay Range Report" and including the job title for which you want information. Along with the letter, send a copy of your résumé, a detailed description of the job, and payment (which can be in the form of a personal check, a major credit card number along with the expiration date, or a corporate pay order). You can compose your own job description, send a formal job description provided by an organization, or use the posting/advertisement announcing an opening. The more complete and detailed the information you provide about the job and your qualifications, the more accurate and specific the "Pay Range Report" will be. In most cases, you will receive your report within a week.

Finally, business periodicals often contain information on the salaries and employment terms in particular fields, industries, and geographical areas. Look under "salaries" in any of the indexes of business periodicals previously cited.

Industries and Companies

General references.   Your first step in getting information on industries and companies should be to spend some time with:

Business Information Sources, 2d ed. Lorna Daniells (Berkeley: University of California Press, 1985).

Daniells, a research librarian at Harvard Business School, organizes business information into 20 broad categories, each of which is treated in a separate chapter. There are chapters, for example, on "Locating information on companies, organizations and individuals," "Industry statistics," and "Marketing." In each chapter, Daniells reviews and evaluates specific information sources, including books, handbooks, periodicals, directories, and on-line data bases. You may also want to consult the:

Encyclopedia of Business Information Sources by Paul Wasserman (Detroit: Gale Research, revised irregularly).

This volume is organized according to specific subjects, such as Aluminum Industry, Chief Executive Officers, Financial Ratios, and Nuclear Power. These two books, at least one of which you can find in almost every library, will direct you to the specific sources of information you need.

Annual reports.   Whenever possible, you should take a look at a company's annual report before going to an informational or selection interview. Annual reports are available for all publicly owned companies, which sell stock and must report on their activities to shareholders. A phone call to the Public Affairs, Public Relations, or Investor Relations Department is generally all it takes to get one mailed to you. Annual reports are also available at many local libraries on microfiche. These reports present companies in the most favorable light possible and do not include the most up-to-date information, so you should consult other, more objective, critical, and current sources to evaluate a company's suitability for you. Annual reports do, however, give you a good feeling for how a company wishes to be seen and will usually provide an overview of the services and products the company produces, as well as of the direction in which the company is headed.

Privately owned companies and nonprofit organizations may or may not publish annual reports and are somewhat harder to research. *Dun & Bradstreet (D&B) Business Information Reports* are often cited as good sources of information on privately held companies, but they are not available through libraries—only other businesses can get them, and businesses who subscribe to the service are not supposed to make reports available for employment purposes. You may, however, be able to get copies of the reports you seek through your local bank—many banks subscribe to the D&B service to help evaluate the creditworthiness of companies seeking loans. Alternatively, you may be able to persuade a businessperson you know to help you get reports if his or her employer subscribes to the service or regularly requests individual reports. Reports costs from $19 to $60 apiece, so you may have to shell out some money. My advice is that you skip this source unless you are desperate to get information about a company, are extremely eager to work there, and cannot find any other source of information.

Government sources. The Small Business Administration (SBA) is a good source of information on small businesses. This federal agency provides a service called the "Answer Desk," which is accessible through a toll-free number (800-827-5722). By phoning the "Answer Desk," you can find out about SBA publications and services and locate the SBA office nearest you. The SBA is a particularly helpful source of information for those thinking about starting their own businesses.

Universities all over the country host Small Business Development Centers; check with the universities in your region to see if one is located nearby. These centers, which are affiliated with the SBA, are generally excellent sources of information, and most are willing to share what they have with people not associated with the university.

Periodicals. Fortunately, the recent surge of interest in small businesses has spawned a variety of periodical publications that focus on them. To locate relevant articles, consult the following indexes of business periodical literature, one or more of which you can find in most libraries:

Business Index
Business Periodicals Index
Wall Street Journal Index
Predicasts F&S Indexes

All of the above indexes allow you to access information through both company names and subject areas and are helpful in locating information on all kinds of business organizations—large or small; public, private, or nonprofit. Browsing through them will also acquaint you with some of the major business periodicals devoted to particular industries. Be sure to look for articles on companies at which you plan to do any sort of interviewing. Nothing will damage the credibility of your interest in a company faster than not having read the recent cover feature in *Business Week* or *Forbes* on that company. Many librarians also keep files or notebooks containing clippings from local newspapers on local businesses—these can be godsends when trying to locate information on smaller businesses not likely to be written up in national publications.

Industry overviews.   For industry overviews, the best sources of information are Standard & Poor's *Industry Surveys*, a quarterly publication, and Wasserman's *Encyclopedia of Business Information Sources*, which was cited previously. Both are widely available in the business sections of larger libraries.

Individuals

All of the information sources discussed so far will help you identfy important decision makers in organizations. Annual reports list a company's officers and sometimes profile workers in a variety of positions. Articles in business periodicals will often mention several people within the company featured, and many periodicals carry articles about individual people. As you read about an organization that interests you, note the names and titles of people mentioned. Then, if you decide to seek employment there, write to those individuals and mention the article in which they were featured—few people are entirely immune to appeals to vanity.

Generally, all you need do to get the address and phone number of someone within an organization is to call the central switchboard. Simply say you have some material to send to the person in question and want to make sure you have the right address.

In addition to these sources, you can consult references specifically geared to supplying information on individuals. These include a vast array of Who's Whos—there are Who's Whos of women in business, people in government, people in education, people in consulting, people from a variety of ethnic or racial backgrounds in a variety of organizations, etc. One of the most helpful is *Who's Who in Finance and Industry*. See what your library has to offer and consult the reference librarian about the most likely sources of information on given individuals.

Also helpful are:

Standard & Poor's Register of Corporations, Directors and Executives, which lists key executives and directors for over 3000 companies.

Contacts Influential: Commerce and Industry Directory (San Francisco: Market Research and Development Services, updated frequently).

How to Reach Anyone Who's Anyone by Michael Levine. (Los Angeles: Price/Stern/Sloan).

Chapter Five

Getting Interviews

In general, getting employment interviews requires creating a résumé, composing cover letters, and making phone calls. You may make your initial request for an interview over the phone or through a letter; you may or may not send a résumé along with each letter or after each phone call, but at some point along the way you will need a résumé and you will have to write letters and make phone calls. I emphasize the need for using all three forms of communication during the interview process because some advisers these days frown on résumés, recommending a number of less traditional, substitute documents or even suggesting that résumés and similar documents be bypassed completely. Some job seekers, on the other hand, seem to think that a résumé is the only form of communication required for gaining interviews and give little thought to cover letters or follow-up phone calls.

The résumé's strength and usefulness in the selection process comes largely from the fact that it is a standardized, traditional form of self-presentation. Most people in organizations are accustomed to looking at résumés, expect to see them from job candidates, and find them helpful in screening, interviewing, and comparing candidates. If you are asked for a résumé and reply that you do not have one or do not believe in them or produce something that bears little resemblance to a résumé, you will look unprofessional or obnoxious, unless you are a damn good talker. My advice is to create a résumé that sticks closely to standard formats, and to supplement your résumé with strong cover letters and effective phone calls.

CREATING A RÉSUMÉ

Résumé Rule 1: Keep your résumé brief, its layout simple, and its type-faces readable: make it visually easy to scan.

As you design your résumé, remember that it is meant to: (1) be read quickly, (2) give an overview of your career (i.e., any aspect of your life relevant to the work you are seeking), (3) facilitate comparison of candidates, (4) supply topics for further discussion in interviews, and (5) serve as an extended self-introduction. It is not meant to get you a job. Final candidate selection depends more on interviews than on résumés, so you do not have to squeeze every fact of your work life into your résumé. If you can fit your résumé on a page, great, but do not cram your material on the page using skimpy margins and small type. Better to go with two pages than to create one page that will strain your readers' eyes and patience.

Résumé Rule 2: Do not include "personal" information on your résumé.

Your résumé should not contain any information that should be irrelevant to the selection process, like your marital status, height, weight, age, number of children, and religion. A surprising number of people still put such information on résumés, even though employers are barred by law from considering it in employment decisions. Some people include it simply because this kind of information was once standard on résumés; others include it because they think it will work to their advantage.

Beware, however. Even if you think, for example, that being married will be a selling point (and in some organizations, it may be, especially for men), do not include your marital status on your résumé. First, you simply do not know how any given reader will react to your married state. Some may view marriage as an impediment to long hours, travel, and job commitment rather than an inducement to stability, loyalty, and productivity. Second, you will look unprofessional because such information is no longer considered appropriate on résumés.

Résumé Rule 3: Use a basically chronological pattern of organization but introduce elements from other résumé formats as needed to suit your particular situation.

Information on résumés is traditionally arranged in reverse chronological order under broad headings such as "Experience" and "Education." Dates are presented in a prominent place—often at the left margin—to enable readers to get an overview of your career quickly. The chronological format is sometimes termed an *obituary résumé* because it focuses on the past, describing work in terms of start and end dates, job titles, duties and responsibilities, and employers' names and addresses.

To avoid the static tone, backward-looking focus, and emphasis on smooth career transition of chronological résumés, some experts recommend using a *functional* format. At their best, functional résumés feature skills, qualifications, and accomplishments and focus on what candidates will be able to do for prospective employers, rather than on what they have done for past employers. Unfortunately, functional résumés have a bad reputation in the business world. Many people use them precisely because they obscure gaps, discontinuities, and anomalies in careers, which makes readers immediately suspicious of résumés in the functional format.

Standard information tends to be harder to find in functional résumés, which makes them more difficult to evaluate and to compare with other résumés. I've read some functional résumés two and three times carefully without being able to get a clue, for example, about how many years of experience the writer has in a particular area. When readers face dozens or hundreds of résumés, any that are not immediately intelligible tend to go onto the "no" pile early in the selection process. The emphasis on skills and accomplishments in functional résumés often comes at the expense of more factual and verifiable information about where and how long the candidate has used given skills and the contexts in which accomplishments were forged.

Functional résumés find favor among candidates who actually have little verifiable experience and expertise or whose experience lies primarily outside the field in which they are seeking work. Because of the strong suspicion of functional résumés, however, such candidates simply throw themselves a second strike by calling attention to possible weaknesses through use of a functional format. The functional format first became popular during the 1960s and 70s, when many women decided to reenter the work force after years of raising children and managing households. Women in this situation perceived themselves (realistically, I'm afraid) as being at a disadvantage compared with candidates whose work careers stretched without interruption from graduation to the present. How were these women to communicate the skills, knowledge, and characteristics acquired during years of work outside corporate settings—at home, in community organizations, and in local schools—through the rigid format of a traditional, chronological résumé? The functional résumé emerged as the answer.

A better answer at this point for nontraditional job seekers is to use a basic chronological pattern with modifications. Think of the chronological format as a frame into which you can fit any kind of experience. One of the most impressive résumés I've ever seen was prepared by a woman with a master's degree in education who spent 15 years raising two sons, managing the finances and day-to-day operations of a household that included her semi-invalid father-in-law, and participating in various community activities. She described each of these areas of experience in a separate entry, following the conventions of chronological presentation. Within each entry, she described her work in terms of transferable skills such as ability to define objectives, solve problems, give directions, recover from setbacks, maintain composure in stressful situations, manage time, set priorities, coordinate the activities of others, and tolerate interruptions. The resulting résumé conveyed a sense of humor as well as a wealth of other managerial skills.

Another departure from the traditional chronological format is the *targeted résumé*. This format is designed to highlight qualifications for a particular position in a particular organization. It generally follows a broadly chronological pattern but emphasizes experiences most directly related to the requirements of a specific opening in a given organization or kind or organization like a large bank, a public university, or a new biotech venture. Experiences not closely related to the targeted position may be listed without elaboration, listed in a separate section devoted to "other experience," or omitted entirely.

In some respects, every résumé should be targeted, emphasizing experience and schooling most directly relevant to the kind of work you seek. I urge you, however, to think of your cover letters as the documents designed to relate your background to particular positions in particular organizations. If you try to do specific targeting in your résumé, you will have to do a new version for each job you seek, and you may face a credibility problem. Readers are apt to wonder how accurate a picture your résumé presents if it is obviously a picture cropped and retouched to match a particular job. You may also define yourself too narrowly and miss out on other opportunities in the organizations you have targeted. When readers are impressed by your résumé but cannot hire you for some reason, they will often circulate your résumé to others. A well-targeted résumé may turn into a liability in such situations.

Résumé Rule 4: In describing previous jobs and educational experiences, focus on accomplishments and transferable skills.

Use a brief prose description of daily duties and responsibilities for each job to introduce a list of accomplishments. Make sure both description and list convey transferable skills. A chronological format demands only that you unfold your experience in a simple, easy-to-follow pattern of organization; it does not require you to stick to static, formalistic descriptions of jobs or schooling.

If you have done your homework in self-exploration, you will have already analyzed your career in terms of accomplishments and transferable skills. To translate this information into résumé format, prepare a separate piece of paper or 4" × 6" card for each job you have had and each school you have attended. Give yourself 10 to 15 minutes for each job or school to rough out a general description of the experience. Then turn to your accounts of accomplishments and skills. Under the prose description of each experience, list the relevant accomplishments and skills.

Résumé Rule 5: Do not try to mold your experience into résumé format too quickly.

Even if you already have a reasonably current version of your résumé around, don't think in terms of revising it. Instead, think in terms of building a new résumé. Like all construction projects, the construction of a résumé takes time and should proceed in steps. The result of a well-managed project will be a high-quality résumé that will help you achieve your present career objectives, and in the process of constructing it, you will help yourself prepare intellectually and emotionally for interviews.

When you have completed a separate sheet or card for each major vocational experience, spread them all out in front of you (you may need to get down on you knees and use the floor for this step). Group them in reverse chronological order under two major subdivisions: Work experience and Education. Reread all of your cards or papers to get a sense of how your career sounds in this pattern of organization. Look for repetition and patterns of advancement. You will want to highlight advancements (increasing levels of skill, responsibility, accomplishment, and reward) while eliminating unnecessary repetition.

You need not, for example, describe your involvement in budgeting under each and every job, if your last three jobs have all involved formulating budgets and tracking expenses and revenues. On the other hand, if your last three jobs have involved increasing responsibility for budgets—a progression, perhaps from providing information to others who formulate budgets to managing the budgeting process across several departments—make sure your descriptions convey this progression.

As you edit your job and school descriptions, keep your current vocational objective securely in mind. If you are seeking jobs in which budgetary responsibilities will be few or nonexistent, you have nothing to gain by emphasizing this aspect of your previous experience. You may wish to use it, however, to demonstrate transferable skills required in budgeting, like ability to work with numbers, explain calculations to others, negotiate for resources, or use a variety of software packages.

Résumé Rule 6: Use a computer and laser printer, if at all possible, to create the master copy of your résumé.

When and only when you have assembled a complete set of descriptions should you begin thinking about page layout or transferring information onto a page. Now is the point at which to bring on the electronics. A computer is a big asset in constructing résumés and creating other business documents useful during vocational transition. Try to get access to one at this point, if you haven't already. A personal computer is a reasonable investment for any manager or professional seeking work. Having résumé information on computer makes it much easier to manipulate and revise, both visually and verbally. Also, computer-generated and laser-printed documents now set the standards against which other documents are compared. Typewritten résumés just do not look very good next to résumés created with sophisticated word-processing software and printing hardware.

If you do not want to invest in a personal computer setup, you can lease computer time or hire a résumé service or independent word processor who uses personal computers. Having your résumé on disk makes sense even if you don't own a computer. You can have your disk printed out wherever you can find the right kind of computer and software attached to a high-quality printer. Computer facilities are all over the place, so you will almost always have access to means of generating a fresh original of your résumé, which you can photocopy, if necessary. Check the yellow pages and the advertising sections of local newspapers to locate the computer resources and expertise you decide to buy.

Résumé Rule 6a: Don't get carried away by technology.

Just because you *can* use 20 different fonts almost as easily as one doesn't mean you *should*. Keep your page visually simple and consistent; use format and layout devices sparingly to achieve emphasis. Do not introduce new design elements for the sake of variety alone.

Résumé Rule 7: Get rid of extraneous lines and subheadings.

Many résumés waste space on unnecessary lines like:

"Résumé of:" (which should be obvious).

"References available on request" (of course they are, but they usually are not requested until the final stages of selection and hiring; you should generally wait for the subject to come up in interviews before offering to supply references).

Full addresses of employers and schools represent another space-eater in résumés. City and state is enough. No one should get in touch with former employers or schools before talking to you; few will want to in any case.

Sometimes résumés waste space and look cluttered because of unnecessary subdivision. For example, "Experience in Advertising," "Experience in Marketing," and "Other Experience" need not appear on the same résumé. Experience, Education, and Additional Information are, in the majority of cases, the only major subdivisions and subheadings a résumé needs. You should describe all your work experiences in terms that show their relevance to your employment objective, so dividing your work background into "Experience in . . ." and "Other Experience" is superfluous.

Likewise, you should not subdivide your experience into "Paid Employment" and "Volunteer Work." This subdivision is not very useful in evaluating your ability to do a job. Volunteering demonstrates community involvement, high energy, and moral fibre—important aspects of character. But dividing your experience into "volunteer work" and "paid employment" only obscures the continuities and coherence in your career path. Stick with a chronological pattern under the single heading of "experience." If you want, you can indicate your pay status within individual entries. If you decide to include voluntary work on your résumé, but do not want it in the "Experience" section, describe or list it under "Additional Information."

Résumé Rule 8: Include an "Additional Information" section—or equivalent—in your résumé.

A flexible heading can introduce a rich and unique variety of information to readers of your résumé. A section of this sort gives the chronological résumé far more latitude as a means of self-introduction. You can include in it information that does not fit neatly into job descriptions and identify activities you do not have space to describe in separate entries. You can mention interests outside of work that you feel demonstrate work-related qualities, like jogging, aerobics, an interest in current events or archaeology, reading books, and volunteering for community activities. Or, you can indicate proficiency with software, hardware, or foreign languages that you have not mentioned in your job descriptions.

Use two criteria to decide whether to include a piece of information on your résumé. First, is it relevant to your employment objective? Second, is it something you want to elaborate on in interviews? If the answer to both is "yes," including the information on your résumé is appropriate.

Résumé Rule 9: Look at all the résumés you can get your hands on, particularly from people in your field.

Libraries and bookstores usually carry a variety of manuals and workbooks on résumé-writing. Most of these contain samples. In addition to general résumé books, you can find volumes devoted to résumés in particular fields. Some librarians even collect sample résumés from satisfied patrons. Gather résumés from friends, family members, and business associates. Look at many before you decide on a look that suits you.

Résumé Rule 10: Proofread your résumé at least 10 times, including each and every proper name and address, especially your own; then have it proofread at least twice by others before having it reproduced or sending it to a potential employer.

Mistakes in résumés always leave a bad impression. Some people will read your résumé and not be able to remember immediately afterward whether you have an M.B.A.; yet, they will recall for years to come the spelling error in your third entry. Don't let nitpickers get your dander up. Beat them to the point and pick that nit out of your résumé before they have a chance at it.

COMPOSING COVER LETTERS

Use cover letters to reveal your uniqueness and to show how your assets meet the particular needs of a particular organization. Broadcast cover letters—those designed to cover your résumé to dozens of different organizations—are largely a waste of time. A cover letter should be a personal letter, and the bad reputation cover letters sometimes have among managers stems from the fact that most of the ones they see are of the broadcast variety. Not surprisingly, most get tossed into the wastebasket with little more than a glance—sometimes less. However, *a well-written, tar-*

geted, and personal cover letter will always be read and sometimes does more to get your foot in the door than an impressive résumé.

A cover letter has two closely related functions to perform. First, it introduces you and your résumé to a person in an organization at which you are seeking employment. Second, it requests an interview. How well your interview request is received depends largely on how well you introduce yourself through your letter and résumé. The more persuasively you present yourself as a candidate for particular work that meets the needs of a particular organization, the better your chances of winning an interview.

Your résumé provides an overview of your career, assets, and accomplishments. Your cover letter should relate the information in your résumé specifically to a job or kind of work for a specific organization. It should implicitly answer three questions for your reader:

1. Why do you want to work for us (or me)?
2. What do you offer that we (or I) need?
3. Why should we (or I) take the time to interview you—What makes you different from hundreds of other candidates for this position (or kind of work)?

Cover Letter Law 1: Write to a person, not to an organization, department, or functional area.

Make your cover letters sound human and give them some personality, preferably some of your own. If at all possible by legal means, get the name of a particular person to whom to address your letter. If you must write to an impersonal entity in answer to advertisements that give no names and forbid calls, imagine writing to someone you know to give your writing a hint of life and voice.

And don't waste much time answering blind or semiblind ads: respond to those you find particularly appealing, but make your effort proportional to the likelihood of payoff—which is slim. Finally, don't give up looking for jobs in organizations that reject you (often without acknowledging receipt of your materials) for advertised openings. Continue networking and researching your way into these organizations in search of other possibilities—and in search of specific individuals with whom to discuss employment possibilities.

Cover Letter Law 2: Keep it to a page and don't simply repeat information from your résumé.

Self-introductions can lose interest fast. Remember that your total self-introduction package will consist of a letter *and* a résumé *and* a phone conversation. You don't have to pack your entire introduction into any one of these communications. Two or three paragraphs of moderate length (averaging three to four sentences in this genre of writing) should give you enough space to say why your background is particularly well suited to a specific kind of work and why you want to work for a particular organization. You won't be able to elaborate, but that is what you hope to do in the interview your cover letter will request.

Cover Letter Law 3: Always request an interview and always end your letter with provisions for following up on your request.

"*Always*" is strong, but there are, truly, very few valid exceptions to this law. Some cover letters begin with requests for interviews:

> I would like to meet with you about working for Zertex as a. . . . My experience for the past four years at ABC has demonstrated my ability to. . . .

Most cover letters save both the request and the action step—the provisions for following up—until the end:

> I would like to talk with you further about work opportunities in marketing at Zertex and will call your office within the week to see if we can arrange a time to meet.

Waiting around for a response is a drag, so don't do it if you don't have to. Take the initiative for following up, and let your reader know how and when you plan to do so. If you are too distant to request a face-to-face meeting, suggest making an appointment for a phone interview and indicate when you will call to make the appointment.

Cover Letter Law 4: Watch your writing style.

Cover letters are hard to write, and writing good ones takes time. You should not feel inadequate as a writer if you find that a single, well-written, and truly personal cover letter takes more than a day to write, particularly at the beginning of your search. With practice, you will probably compose letters more rapidly. As you work on cover letters, however, keep in mind that making the effort to get them looking and sounding good can pay you back many times over.

Finding a writing style that reveals your personality while maintaining a professional tone is a demanding job. One of the major criticisms I hear of cover letters is that the bulk are stiff, dry, formalistic, and difficult to read. Another major criticism is that they lack any sense of enthusiasm or excitement. Both criticisms suggest the same underlying problem—the writer tried too hard (and succeeded all too well) at making the letter sound as impersonal and "businesslike" as possible. To achieve this peculiar and unpleasant effect, writers often pattern cover letters on the business documents with which most of us are, unfortunately, quite familiar—those awful form letters banks and insurance companies are so fond of sending customers or those deadly internal memos that so often fill inboxes. The resulting cover letters are likely to be just as welcome and just as well received as the documents after which they are patterned.

Some people, in an effort to get away from the pretentious, unreadable prose style so mindlessly spawned within bureaucratic organizations, go to the opposite extreme and wind up sounding like Ed McMahon selling insurance through the mail to millions. The prose is lively enough, but its hyperbole and frantic tone generate suspicion and annoyance. Readers tend to think, "If this guy is so great, why does he have to use such a hard sell?" Or, alternatively, they may judge the writer unprofessional because the tone and approach of the letter seem unsuited to the purpose and occasion.

To put your voice into your writing without sacrificing the dignity, precision, and authority that your cover letters should convey, think of composition in two stages. In the first stage, imagine that you are seated across from the person to whom you are writing. Talk to him or her about why you are the best candidate for the work you seek. Use the same kind of language and sentence structure you would use in conversation. No one says—even in the most stilted of business conversations—"As per your ad in last Sunday's employment section. . . ." But many people feel compelled to write this way. Don't. Go instead with a more conversational tone and choice of words like, "I saw your ad in last Sunday's employment section. . . ."

During phase one, write quickly and don't edit; you may find freewriting a helpful technique at this point. You are not aiming for perfection yet, which will come in phase two. Rather, you are aiming to discover your message. To discover your message, you need to explore the question, "What do I need to say about myself to persuade my reader to interview me?" As you write quickly the things that come to mind, you will start to develop a clearer sense of what your cover letter needs to communicate. Message firmly in mind, you can select the material most germane to getting it across persuasively. Once again, the key to creating masterpieces is to generate material in quantity, from which you can select the best, thus arriving at quality.

Before the second stage of writing, give yourself a substantial break— go take a walk, do the dishes, or make some phone calls. Stage two requires distance and objectivity. When you return from your break, edit your first draft systematically—not by ear alone. Look for potential reading problems: words, phrases, and passages that may require more than a single reading to comprehend. Among the potential problems to search for are:

- Long sentences, especially several in a row.
- Series of short, choppy sentences.
- Repetitious use of words or sentence patterns (in cover letters, it is particularly important to check the beginning of each sentence and paragraph; if each begins with "I," you need to do some work).
- Over use of passive voice.
- Dangling modifying phrases (e.g., "Having read the article in last week's *Forbes*, Zertex, Inc. appeals to me more than ever because . . .").
- Heavy use of technical jargon and acronyms.
- Loosely structured paragraphs that skip or shift from topic to topic with no apparent unifying theme.
- Errors in punctuation and usage.

If the above list leaves you scratching your head, trying to remember how your freshman composition teacher defined *passive voice* or wondering what constitutes a dangerously long sentence, take the time to review the basics of writing style. Almost any good book on writing will do.

Cover Letter Law 5: After you have composed and edited a letter, rewrite the first paragraph.

The opening of any communication—whether a letter, memo, phone conversation, or interview—sets the stage for what follows. A false or a slow start may prevent you from winning—or even finishing—the race. You need to get and focus your reader's attention in the first paragraph, and you cannot do either effectively if you use it as a warm-up exercise. Frequently, the best opening sentences get buried in the middle of letters, where it's often too late for them to have much impact. When you have finished a cover letter, look through it for the most arresting, assertive sentence. It will probably be at the end of your second or third paragraph. Disinter it and move it to the start of your letter. Then rewrite the rest of the first paragraph, if necessary, and patch up the paragraph from which you took your opening sentence. Below are examples of buried sentences that added life and interest to letters when moved to the beginning:

> I could help Zertex meet its challenging marketing goals, just as I helped Megamoney University increase its applicants by 75 percent in just two years.
>
> I can cut your costs without cutting quality.
>
> Zertex wants innovators, and my career is one of turning bright ideas into profitable projects.
>
> Fifteen years in project management have shown my ability to make groups into teams and to make teams into winners.

The ultimate impact of a good start depends, of course, on what follows. A strong opening can look pretty limp when the follow-through is weak. If you make an assertive claim about yourself in your first sentence, you must back it up with facts. If you say you can cut costs without compromising quality, you had better give at least one example of quantifiable, verifiable gains in productivity due to your efforts. Don't try to back up an assertion with hype or with additional general claims about your abilities and accomplishments.

Cover Letter Law 6: Use good-quality and relatively conservative stationery that matches your résumé.

Almost every book and every expert encourages job seekers to use a medium weight paper for cover letters, to select a kind that matches the feel and color of the résumé, and to stick with shades of white or slightly off white. Yet, some job seekers feel amazingly insecure about excellent stationery and others disregard time-honored advice in favor of lavender, scented paper, hoping to stand out from the crowd. Either extreme is silly. If you are using a good-quality, medium weight bond that is white or not far from it, you are fine. Stop worrying about trivia and get on with your job search.

If you are considering paper that is blue, yellow, pink, gray, or green, forget it. Graphic designers may be able to use more colorful and interesting papers, but most other folks should stick to boring old white (or slightly off white). You will not get noticed in an advantageous way by using colored stationery. I don't know of anyone who has been asked for an interview—much less offered a job—based on an unusual choice of stationery. Do you?

TELEPHONE TECHNIQUE

Telephoning can be torture. Frustrations to communication lurk behind every call: the palace guards whose job is to prevent you from disturbing the boss, the voice-mail systems from which there are no exits, the phone-answering machines whose owners use them to avoid all human contact, the operators who transfer your calls to the moon while disclaiming all knowledge of any department or person you might be seeking. Telephone tag has become a national pastime, and there are some very fast players in almost every organization. Your mission is to play their game and beat them at it. But only when necessary.

Telephone Tip 1: Be persistent; do not call yourself out until after at least three strikes.

Use three as a magic number to condition yourself to repeating your request at least three times to everyone you contact in a game of phone tag before accepting a "no." Usually you should not repeat your request verbatim; instead, your task is more complex. You will try at least three times to reach your goal by alternative routes, which may require modifying your original request or figuring out how to rephrase it so that it is more clearly understood. Whether your goal is to get a phone number or an appointment, take three no's before giving up.

Suppose you call Zertex to get the number of the marketing director profiled in a recent magazine article on the company. You sent him a letter and résumé and you are now following up. You dial the number for Zertex given in your local phone book and reach an operator at the central information desk. You ask for James Williams.

"Just a moment. . . . I'm sorry, we have no one by that name here." Silence. (1st no)

"Could you please check again? I'm almost certain you have a number for him." (2nd try)

"All right, but I'm certain I won't find anything I didn't find two seconds ago." A very long pause. "No. No James Williams and no Jim Williams." (2nd no)

"Well, perhaps you could help me locate him—or whomever might have taken his position. I need to speak with the director of marketing. Could you give me a number for the marketing department?" (3rd try)

"The receptionist at that department can be reached at xxx-xxxx." Not exactly a strike, but definitely a foul tip. So you try again.

"Could you also give the name and address of the director?"

"His name is—let me see—John Williams (the voice sounds annoyed, but it is providing the information). His address is Marketing Department, 23rd Floor, Northwest Wing. Could he be the man you're looking for?" Finally—you've made it to first base.

"Maybe. I read about him in an article and I'm sure they used 'Jim,' but could you give me the number?"

"John Williams is at xxx-xxxx. Have a good day."

"Thank you for your help."

Some of your maneuvers in telephone tag games will be nothing more than a means of buying time to figure out your next move. In the above dialogue, for example, asking the operator to recheck the directory for a listing is essentially a way to buy time. During this time, the caller is able to regroup her thoughts. She wants to talk to the director of marketing about employment at Zertex and needs to be able to contact his office to make an appointment. Whether Jim Williams is still the director makes little difference at this point, so she decides to find a way to reach the marketing department, from which she will doubtless be able to discover who is in charge of marketing. If it is someone other than Jim Williams, she will have to decide whether to write another letter before seeking an appointment or to seek one immediately.

Telephone Tip 2: Consider every live human you contact during phone forays as a potential ally and source of helpful information.

Callers often make the mistake of viewing anyone who is not the intended recipient of their messages as enemies or simply as barriers to be gotten around. As a result, many callers become angry, pompous, impatient, demanding, and rude with the very people who can be most helpful in finding ways into an organization. You can learn a great deal about an organization from the people who stand between you and the person you want to reach, and the information you gather may be useful in crafting your strategy for generating a job offer. In addition, you may need to go through the same people repeatedly as you move along in the selection process, and you are at a great advantage compared with other job seekers if the middle people are on your side.

Having a number of stock questions to haul out if you feel blocked by a middle person helps in avoiding frustrating encounters. Anticipating a variety of off-putting responses also helps. Never expect to sail smoothly through corporate channels of communication; always anticipate rough waters, dead calms, and tricky currents—that way you won't be as tempted to abandon your voyage when you hit treacherous waters. Below are a list of questions and responses that often come in handy:

- "When is the best time to catch Mr. or Ms. Alwaysout?"
- "Is there anyone there whom you would suggest I contact instead of (or in addition to) Mr./Ms. AO?"
- "Perhaps you would be willing to help me. I've been trying to get in touch with Ms./Mr. AO for two weeks, and he/she doesn't seem to be responding to my messages. I'd be grateful for any suggestions or help you could provide."
- "Could I at least make a tentative appointment to see him/her? I'll call you back at the end of the week to make sure its OK."
- "I hate to keep bugging you—I know you must be getting tired of taking messages from me—so could you suggest a way for me to get to talk with Mr./Ms. AO for just three minutes?"
- "Do you think it would be a good idea for me to write to Ms./Mr. AO and then call him; or would it be better for me to speak with him briefly over the phone first and follow up with a letter if appropriate?"

Telephone Tip 3: Keep as calm and relaxed during phone conversations as possible and take frequent breaks to loosen up physically.

Many people don't realize how tense they become in phone conversations until the end of the day, when they have splitting headaches, sore shoulders, and upset stomachs. To minimize such unpleasant symptoms of phone fatigue and to keep your voice sounding alert and positive, learn to register and respond to early warning signs of tension. If your neck and shoulders feel tight, get up and do some stretching exercises. If your vocal cords and facial muscles begin to tense up, yawn once or twice and take a break of a few minutes to breathe from the diaphragm.

One of the best ways to improve your telephone personality while reducing tension is to walk and gesture as you talk. Verbal and nonverbal fluency go together. People are slower in selecting and articulating words when stationary than when in motion. In addition, a stationary speaker usually has a static voice—one with little variation in pitch, tone, pace, or volume. Variations communicate emotions, including enthusiasm, warmth, excitement, involvement, and interest; without them, your voice sounds dead.

A related phone technique is to keep a mirror handy for periodically checking your facial expression. Literally put a smile on your face before making each call. The physical act of smiling can change both your voice and your mood. During calls, check your expression occasionally, looking for furrows, frowning, and tightened lips. Again, physically adjusting your facial expression can help you act the mood you want to project and may even change your mood to conform to your more relaxed expression.

Telephone Tip 4: When you leave a message—whether on a machine or with a person—leave your number as a matter of courtesy but keep the initiative for calling back on your side of the line.

Some telemarketing mavens take this piece of advice a step further and counsel against ever leaving a number. They reason that leaving a number leaves you open to getting an important call-back at a time when you are psychologically and intellectually unprepared to do your best. They are right—there's nothing more unnerving than having the important person you've been trying to reach all week call you back just as you return from a jog or emerge from the shower. But never leaving your number puts you in the position of initiating a game of phone tag and does not give the person on the other end of the line the opportunity to call at a time that is psychologically and otherwise good for him or her. Additionally, not giving a number may seem discourteous or unprofessional, especially if you are specifically asked to leave one.

On the other hand, never expect calls to be returned simply because you have left a number. Instead, provide your number but also indicate your intention to call back at a given time or within a specific interval: "This is Mary Caye at xxx-xxxx. I'm calling to follow up on the letter I sent last week and would like to arrange a time to meet with you. I'll try calling again later today." When you follow through as promised and still get an answering machine or intermediary, do not give up (remember the magic number, three). Again leave a message and indicate that you plan to call the following day or early the following week. If you are talking with an intermediary, ask when a call would most likely get through.

Telephone Tip 5: The early bird often gets the worm.

When you have repeatedly tried to reach someone during normal business hours (which vary from industry to industry) without success, try
calling a half hour before or after normal hours. You may, of course, risk
interrupting time set aside for desk work or collection of wits, but if you
acknowledge the possible inconvenience good naturedly, you will usually
get beyond ill humor quickly. For example, you might say quite honestly, "I'm glad I was able to reach you. I know I'm probably disturbing
the only quiet moment of your day, but I'm very eager to talk with you
and promise not to take more than a few minutes of your time." Then
keep your promise—even if the other person seems eager to go beyond
five minutes, bring the call to a close. "I really appreciate the time you've
given me, but I promised not to take too much of it. So I'd like to break
now and set up a time for us to meet in person."

Weekends and holidays are also good times to try contacting elusive
people on your list.

*Telephone Tip 6: When making sales calls (as opposed to informational
calls) keep the telemarketer's ratio in mind: 40:20:5:1.*

That is, expect to make at least 40 phone contacts to locate 20 people who
will actually talk with you over the phone (the other 20 will say no
through intermediaries, be perpetually unreachable, or simply stonewall
you with something like, "No, we're not doing any hiring now, and we
don't anticipate doing any for the remainder of the year, and no, I won't
talk to you any further, so goodbye!"). Of the 20 who do speak with you,
only 5 will agree to see you. From 5 employment interviews, you can
expect to generate 1 solid prospect of employment, which usually means
a call-back for further interviewing, rarely an offer.

Many salespeople recommend viewing no's as part of the selling process, suggesting that you see each no as a step toward a yes. Keeping the
telemarketer's ratio in mind helps you maintain some perspective on your
failures: no matter how good your telephone technique, you should not
expect to beat the 40:20:5:1 ratio. If you do beat it, wonderful; you've won
the lottery. But don't underestimate the work, time, or difficulty involved
in closing a sale, and don't doubt your competence when half the people
you reach by phone refuse to provide any help or encouragement.

Also, use the ratio to help develop a realistic timetable for obtaining
employment. If you make four phone contacts a day (which will certainly

involve making two or three times as many attempts), it will take two weeks of steady phone work to generate five interview appointments. Initial interviews are generally screening interviews whether you meet with line or staff personnel, and if you pass through the screen, you can count on having several more interviews, possibly spanning several weeks, before receiving a definite no or a job offer. Rarely is the sales cycle for employment shorter than two months, so count on an interval of at least 10 weeks between the time you set up your first employment interviews and the time you learn the outcome of you efforts.

Telephone Tip 7: Always try for a face-to-face meeting, whether your goal is getting information or getting a job.

Use the telephone primarily as a vehicle for literally getting your foot in the door. Even if you are told that no openings are anticipated in the foreseeable future, keep plugging: tell your contact that you would still like to find out more about the ABC Organization and ask him or her to meet with you for just 10 minutes. Promise, if necessary, not to discuss employment during your meeting. Most people are willing to give up 10 minutes, especially if they do not feel pressured to respond to a bid for employment.

Also, most people are more generous with information and advice when facing another live, breathing human than over the phone with a stranger. If you promise not to push the employment issue, don't. But you will often find that the "no" is more tentative and conditional in person than over the phone. It is not unusual, for example, for a contact to reintroduce the employment question, if you make a good impression in person. However, when you win an interview by promising a 10-minute time limit, take responsibility for fulfilling your promise. Bring the interview to a close after 10 minutes and try to arrange another meeting, if that seems desirable and appropriate.

When interviewing for information, it may often seem easier to conduct the interview over the phone than in person. But try for a face-to-face meeting anyway. You will get more information and build a more committed set of human resources if you make personal contacts. Electronically mediated communication may be the wave of the future, but humans are still human and respond strongly to touch and to facial expressions. A firm handshake and warm expression create a bond that even the most productive and friendly of phone relationships simply cannot duplicate.

FIGURE 8
Phone Log

Day and Date: _____   **Calls to Make:** _____

Time	In/Out	Name and Affiliation	Time Spent	Goal	Comments and Follow-Up

Telephone Tip 8: Before you call, know what you want, be able to articulate it briefly and clearly, and have fall-back positions.

Most people find it helpful to jot down the major points they want to make or questions they want to ask before initiating a call. Imagining possible responses and objections is also helpful so that you can have replies and counterproposals ready to hand. Avoid, however, writing out full scripts—you will invariably want to read your lines, and unless you are a master both at writing dialogue and at acting, your delivery will sound stiff and unnatural.

Do not try to be coy or indirect about your interest in employment, if that is what you want to discuss. Say you are interested in working at ABC and say it with enthusiasm. Never try to get an employment interview by disguising it as a purely informational encounter. If an informational interview turns into an employment interview at the initiative of the interviewer, that's fine. But if you say you are seeking information, stick to seeking information unless your contact brings up the topic of employment. You can , however, ask at the end of an informational interview for names of people with whom to discuss employment or seek advice about the best strategy for getting employment in your informational contact's organization.

Telephone Tip 9: Keep accurate and detailed records of phone transactions.

Note each phone conversation in your contact file and record any agreements reached, information acquired, or follow-up communication that may be appropriate. You may also want to keep a separate phone log like the one illustrated in Figure 8.

Daily phone logs help you monitor your progress and provide good documentation of long-distance calls for tax purposes. They also help you keep your thoughts focused on your objectives as you go through a series of calls. Similarly, they can help you identify patterns of ineffective phoning. If, for example, you notice that you rarely have anything to put in the follow-up column, you probably are not managing your phoning in a way that nurtures continuing contact, and you need to alter your phone strategy. Finally, the phone log habit is an excellent one to acquire for when you return to work.

Chapter Six

Turning Interviews into Job Offers

Interviews play a tremendously large part in hiring decisions, probably much too large. Some studies indicate that managers make better hiring decisions when they have access solely to written materials, such as résumés, application forms, transcripts, and letters of recommendation, than when they have access to both documentation and interviewing or to interviewing alone. The reason this might be so is not hard to figure out: interviews allow a wide variety of personal and social biases to enter the selection process. From documents alone, it is difficult to determine whether an applicant is black or white, tall or short, bulky or trim, a fashionable or conservative dresser, a fast talker or a drawler, stunningly attractive or homely. Such characteristics have nothing to do with the ability to perform most jobs, but they have a great deal to do with the kind of impression an interviewee makes on an interviewer.

First impressions are critical in interviews. Many interviewers claim (with pride!) that they can judge a candidate's suitability for a job within the first minute or two of conversation and that they rarely alter their original judgments based on subsequent interactions. People who make this claim generally attribute their speediness in evaluating others to a highly developed sense of human nature. A far more plausible reason for their failure to alter initial judgments is their inability to process any subsequent information that might call into question their first impressions. Psychologists have shown that once a human has formulated a hypothesis, he or she is likely to interpret all information in a way that supports the hypothesis or to simply disregard any information that might cast doubt on the validity of the hypothesis. We are much more likely to twist information to fit a hypothesis than to alter or discard a hypothesis in light of contradictory information. Hence the absurd but often repeated homily, "It's the exception that proves the rule."

Because the first few minutes of interviews are crucial, and because interviews are crucial to selection decisions, you should prepare yourself psychologically, intellectually, and physically to make a good impression. Preparation is key to good interview performance, in part because it helps you develop the self-confidence that will enable you to make a good first impression and to maintain it throughout a series of interviews. You cannot make biases disappear in the interviewing process, but you may have a great deal more power than you realize to affect the outcome of an interview. Unlocking your power as an interviewee requires two things: an understanding of the interview as a form of communication and diligent preparation.

INTERVIEWS AS CONVERSATIONS

The first point to keep in mind during your preparations is that interviews are forms of conversation. Like any form of conversation, an interview should involve a two-way flow of information. Your interviewer will gather information about you, and you, in turn, should be gathering information about the organization, the job, and the interviewer. View yourself, therefore, as being as much in control of an interview as the interviewer. Do not allow an interview to become an interrogation, which is *not* a form of conversation because the flow of information goes only in one direction.

Interviews are sometimes defined (with some tongue in cheek) as conversations in which two or more people are engaged for some purpose other than the enjoyment of talking with one another.

This definition focuses on the primary distinction between interviews and other forms of conversation—all interviews have a definable purpose other than getting or keeping in touch. In an organizational setting, a counseling interview has as its purpose helping someone define and work through personal problems that affect job performance. A problem-solving interview has as its purpose figuring out how to attack an organizational problem. An informational interview has as its purpose gathering information related to a particular issue or problem. A selection interview has as its purpose assessing the fit between an individual and a job.

One additional distinction generally sets interviews apart from other forms of conversation—interviews are usually time limited. You will generally have to get your message across and gather the information you seek within a fairly strict time frame. Thus, *having an agenda and select-ing the items on it carefully is a prerequisite to top performance.*

DEVELOPING YOUR AGENDA

Think of an agenda as a flexible outline of the points you want to convey about yourself and the questions you want to ask. Flexibility is key. Be-cause you cannot know ahead of time what questions will be asked, you must be flexible in framing the points you want to make in terms that answer questions put to you. This may seem an impossible task, but it is actually much easier than you might think.

When you have an agenda, you will find you are likely to respond to questions with material from it. If you don't have an agenda—if you simply sit in an interview fielding questions as they come along—you are likely to blurt out just about anything in response to an open-ended ques-tion like, "Tell me about yourself." Or, conversely, you are likely to an-swer it by walking your interviewer through your résumé (what a drag). But if you know that one of the major points you want to make about yourself is that you are an excellent team member and leader, you will probably give an answer like:

> I think of myself as basically a team animal. I enjoy working in teams, and I have ever since junior high, when I first became involved in team sports. In college, I put together a team of students to help the administration define its strategy for attracting top students; I both selected the team members and served as the team's leader. As a junior engineer on my first job, I was a member of several project teams and task forces, and always got superior rat-ings from my co-workers and bosses. And in my most recent job, one of the accomplishments of which I feel proudest is turning around a sales team with sagging morale and making it one of the best in the industry. In fact, one of the things that appeals to me most about Zytex is your emphasis on teamwork.

Notice several characteristics of the above answer:

- It is brief compared with most answers to open-ended questions—it takes less than a minute to deliver, even at a relatively slow pace and with the pauses and hesitations characteristic of impromptu speech. A question like, "Tell me about yourself," is likely to come near the beginning of an interview, when you do not want to surpass the limits of your listener's attention with long, rambling answers.

- It is focused on a single theme. It presents information with a point, and the point is clearly stated in the first sentence. Long, discursive answers, while providing a great deal of information, often leave no overall impression and thus take up a great deal of time without having a great deal of impact.
- It relates the information it presents directly to the organization and job being discussed and demonstrates that the candidate has done his or her homework.
- It points the way toward continued questioning by ending on two points that almost beg for elaboration—how the candidate accomplished the turnaround and what else about Zytex the candidate finds attractive. Leading answers are among the interviewee's most powerful tools for shaping an interview.

Without an agenda, you will find it almost impossible to give answers with the above characteristics.

Preparing your agenda for a given interview will involve reviewing the information you have gathered in your research and extracting from it what you believe to be the most salient points about the organization's character and the challenges the organization faces. Write these down.

Next, dig up whatever information you have been able to collect about the position or kind of work the organization offers. This may include a job description and various pieces of information you have gleaned from more general readings and from contacts made while you were setting up the interview. From this information, along with your general knowledge of the organization, prepare a profile of a perfect candidate for the job from the organization's point of view.

Now you are ready to create a "Preparation Sheet" as shown in Figure 9. On this sheet you will first list your assets and liabilities as a candidate for the job. Let's take a look at an example to see how this works. Suppose you are Chris MacKinny, an electronics engineer with experience both in engineering and in selling consulting services. Your last job was as sales manager at a 500-person firm of consulting engineers. You are interviewing for the position of marketing director at Zytex, a midsized (fictional) company that makes and markets bioengineering technology. Your assets might include:

- An engineering background in instrumentation.
- Ability to work well with teams.

FIGURE 9
Preparation Sheet

Assets	Evidence	Liabilities	Compensating Factors

- Five years of experience as sales manager for a consulting engineering firm.
- Strong interest in the emerging field of bioengineering and technology.
- Graduate-level course work in marketing.
- A high energy level.
- Superior analytical and quantitative skills.
- Ability to explain technical concepts simply and clearly.
- Persistence and creativity in tackling complex problems.
- Ability to translate corporate objectives into operational priorities.
- Fluency in Japanese.

On the liability side of the preparation sheet, you might list:

- No experience in marketing as opposed to sales.
- No experience in the specialized bioengineering field.
- Limited experience in strategic planning.
- Involuntary termination of last job and being out of work for eight months.

For each of your assets, you will next list experiences, situations, or accomplishments that demonstrate the validity of your claim to it. For example, "a high energy level" might be demonstrated by: (1) your ability to maintain the productivity of your sales force despite personnel cuts, (2) your active participation in professional associations, and (3) your ability to take demanding courses while maintaining superior performance ratings on your job. Your fluency in Japanese might be shown by having negotiated contracts for engineering projects with Japanese companies and by your extensive travels in Japan during vacations.

Armed with plentiful evidence of your assets, your next job is to convert this evidence into story form. A story is not necessarily fiction; by *story form*, I mean a brief account with a beginning, middle, and end. A story is simply a way of organizing information into a memorable pattern. Your aim is to make you and your assets memorable to interviewers. So, instead of saying that you have traveled extensively in Japan and have been able to make your away around remote areas where nobody else spoke English, you might tell the story of arriving in a small rural village late on a rainy night and managing to talk your way into lodging with a farming family largely because they were amazed to meet an American who could actually speak their language.

You will introduce your stories as a way of elaborating on the points you want to make about yourself. Suppose, for example, in the interview which began with "Tell me a little about yourself," your answer is followed by the question, "What else about Zytex appeals to you?" Your reply might be:

> While researching Zytex, I've noticed that one of your aims is to participate in more joint ventures with Japanese firms. I'd love to have more opportunities to work with the Japanese, and I think my knowledge of the Japanese language and culture would be an invaluable asset to Zytex. In my dealings with the Japanese, I've found that they're very impressed by Americans who actually speak their language and respect their culture. For example, last year while traveling in Japan after a business conference, I arrived at a remote farming village late on a rainy night and found that the inn was closed. But on the way back to the train station, I bumped into a farmer, and he asked in broken English where I was going. He was so amazed to hear me reply in fluent Japanese that after I explained my plight, he invited me to his home to meet his family, share their evening meal, and stay until the inn reopened in the morning.
>
> I think my extensive knowledge of the Japanese can be an invaluable asset, given Zytex's goal of expanding into Japanese markets, and I'd like the opportunity to put it to use.

Formulating stories ahead of time is important; if you rely on your memory and spontaneous story-telling capacity, you will probably tell stories that are too long and get lost on tangents. Also, you will inevitably find that you recall the best stories only after the interview is over.

Finally, remember that experience does not come packaged in story form—this form is what you add to the facts of your experience to give them meaning and to make them memorable. Being invited to stay with a Japanese family means nothing by itself. You must make it mean "ability to work productively with Japanese firms" by making it into a story and putting it into a context that gives the facts the meaning you intend them to have. You should not, however, try to memorize your stories. Your purpose is not to script answers but to make sure that the most salient experiences of your life are at the front of your mind and that you are prepared to talk about them in a focused manner.

What about the liabilities? Do you try desperately to avoid talking about them? Do you try to hide them? Do you lie? None of the above. You prepare to meet them head on. For every liability, you identify compensating factors. You explain how you can overcome your liabilities, showing that they are not insurmountable barriers. At the same time, you will be demonstrating the ability to assess yourself objectively, identify weaknesses, confront them honestly, and overcome them with your strengths. Again, preparation is key. First, you must prepare by identifying the aspects of your background that interviewers for a particular job may take to be shortcomings. This you do when you list your liabilities compared with the perfect candidate for a position.

Next, you use your preparation sheet to list compensating considerations. For example, lack of industry experience is a liability for our friend Chris. But as compensating factors, Chris can list things like:

- A long-standing interest in bioengineering, which has involved following the field and industry closely in trade journals.
- An ability to learn quickly through self-directed study and experience.
- A willingness to pursue formal course work and an ability to do so while fulfilling the requirements of a demanding position.
- Similarities between previous experiences and challenges facing the bioengineering field.
- An ability to bring fresh perspectives to bear on Zytex's problems and opportunities.

Then, you follow the same procedure that you used to substantiate your assets: you list experiences that demonstrate the compensating factors in action, and you develop stories that convey these experiences in a meaningful and memorable manner.

ANTICIPATING QUESTIONS

Interviewers frequently ask questions related to weaknesses. Sometimes the questions will be fairly direct: "What do you take to be your major weaknesses?" Or, "In what areas have you tended to get the lowest marks on your performance evaluations?" At other times, they will be somewhat more subtle and will come in the form of follow-up questions related to incidents you have recounted. In any case, many interviewers will want to explore weaknesses for the obvious purpose of seeing whether you have any that might affect your performance significantly. Perhaps less obvious are underlying concerns about your honesty and your ability to see yourself objectively. Because of these underlying concerns, you should not try to be coy or evasive in supplying answers.

You may have heard the advice that when weaknesses come up in interviews, talk about a weakness that is really the flip side of a strength. "I'm something of a workaholic" or "Sometimes I have unrealistically high expectations of others because I demand so much of myself" are frequently given as examples of such weaknesses. Unless you are talking to an idiot, however, such replies are transparent as attempts to evade serious discussion of the issue. You do not, on the other hand, want to say something that will seriously jeopardize your chances for a job or that will suggest serious problems in the area of self-confidence.

The best way to deal with questions about weaknesses is first to anticipate them—don't be caught off guard when they come up. Second, when filling out your preparation sheet, give serious consideration to those areas in which you probably *are* a weak candidate for a given job compared with other possible candidates. Third, always restrict your discussion of weaknesses to those that are clearly job related and always talk about how you can (or have) compensated for them.

Anticipating questions and possible topics of discussion is an important part of preparing for interviews. Many books and articles give lists of frequently asked questions, and these can be helpful in your preparations. However, you will waste a great deal of time if you try to come up with brilliant answers to the questions on such lists because you will find that few interviewers will be obliging enough to ask any of them in the form for which you have prepared your answers. Also, you will probably have a tendency to script your answers and will either create unnecessary anxiety for yourself in interviews as you try to recall your script, or you will memorize the script with the result that your answers lack spontaneity and sound unnatural.

A better way to anticipate questions is to put yourself in the position of your interviewer. What would you want to know about candidates for a given position? Sit down and list 10 to 15 tough questions you would want to put to yourself if you were the interviewer. As you do so, bear in mind that interviewers often ask questions about major life decisions and transitions because the answers often reveal a great deal about a candidate's process of thinking and acting. They show how candidates have generated and analyzed alternatives, made important decisions, and implemented personal priorities. They reveal something about the candidate's tolerance for risk, ability to recover from setbacks, and capacity for learning from experience. Be sure, therefore, to review each of the major transitions in your work life, beginning with your choice of college. For each, recall what prompted the change, what alternatives you considered, and how and why you decided on the alternative you chose. Also, be prepared for questions designed to reveal how you work with others—bosses, clients, subordinates, and colleagues.

You may also be asked questions aimed at assessing your technical knowledge or skills in specialized areas, especially in the second or third round of interviews, when you are likely to be talking with people in your area of expertise, rather than personnel representatives or general managers. My experience, however, is that most interviewees are amazed and chagrined at how little time is generally spent on technical questions. They are often particularly anxious about such questions—believing they can "wing it" on more general topics—and spend an inordinate amount of time dreaming up incredibly complex questions about technical trivia and trying to frame answers for them. You may be asked such questions, but far less frequently than you may imagine. First of all, in most cases you will not even get to the stage of interviewing for a position unless your credentials strongly suggest that you have the fundamental knowledge and skills the position requires. Second, there are far better means of assessing technical acumen than through interviews (tests, certifications, grades, and the like), and most interviewers will be concerned primarily about getting to know you as a person and as a potential co-worker.

Hypothetical questions are another broad category of questions you should expect to run into in selection interviews. Sometimes called *case questions*, hypothetical questions set out a business situation or problem and ask you how you would tackle it. A hypothetical question in an interview for a consulting position might go something like:

> Suppose a client came to you and said he had excess capacity in his plants and was looking for innovative uses and markets for his product, which is chalk. How would you help the client deal with this problem?

Such questions are among the most challenging to answer, in part because you cannot anticipate what form they may take. They are used most frequently in the consulting industry but are not uncommon in marketing, general management, and many other fields. The most frequent mistake candidates make in trying to answer them is to give too detailed and too final a solution to the problem presented or to panic because they realize they cannot give such an answer. If you don't happen to know anything about chalk or the chalk industry—and most people don't—you, of course, cannot provide a solution to the problem described in the question above. What you can do, however, is provide an approach to attacking the problem.

In answer to hypothetical questions, it is reasonable, therefore, to talk about what kind of information you would want to get about the client and about the industry and how you would use this information in problem solving. You might even discuss the possibility of reformulating the client's perception of the problem to broaden or narrow its definition. As you answer, remember that the interviewer is trying to learn more about your analytical abilities, ability to think on your feet, and your imagination. She or he is not interested in your ability to solve problems of chalk companies. If you anticipate interviewing for consulting jobs, positions in strategic planning, or in marketing management, read any of Michael Porter's books on industry and competitive analysis. Porter, a Harvard Business School professor, presents many very helpful analytical tools and approaches that are invaluable in fielding hypothetical questions.

INTERVIEWING STYLES

Equally important as anticipating questions is anticipating different interviewing styles. You can feel extremely uncomfortable in an interview if your interviewer adopts a style for which you are unprepared. You cannot, of course, know how an interviewer will behave until you get to the interview. You can, however, be aware of the most common kinds of interviewing styles so that you can identify your interviewer's approach and respond appropriately. You have little to gain and much to lose by trying to fight your interviewer's style, which sometimes happens when a candidate feels baffled by an interviewer's strategy and manner.

The Directed Interview

In this kind of interview, as its name suggests, the interviewer directs the interview through a series of relatively closed questions that have been determined beforehand. Generally, the same set of questions is put to every candidate, and the questions tend to stick closely to the facts of each candidate's background. Although relatively rarely used in interviewing candidates for managerial and professional positions, you may run into a directed interview during initial screening. The purpose of a directed interview is to collect the same kind of information from a variety of candidates to facilitate their comparison.

In a sense, a directed interview is the easiest sort to give and to get. Your job is basically to supply information clearly and succinctly, keeping elaboration to a minimum.

The Undirected Interview

The opposite of a directed interview, the undirected interview gives the candidate the widest latitude to present his or her case on his or her own terms. It is characterized by open-ended questions such as, "Tell me a little about yourself," "Tell me more about your work with ABC, Inc.," "Describe your relationship with your last boss," and "Why did you decide to go back to school for your MBA?" In fact, some interviewers will start with a question like, "What can I do for you today?" or "What brings you here today?" The interviewer may have identified certain areas of your background and particular issues to cover but does not have a set of specific questions prepared beforehand. Often, the interviewer takes cues from the interviewee, crafting questions based on previous responses.

If you are well prepared, you can shine in an undirected interview because you will have wide latitude to cover the points on your agenda. If you are poorly prepared, on the other hand, you will probably find undirected interviews unnerving. If the interviewer is not giving the interview direction and you arrive with little sense of direction, you will feel as if you and the interview are drifting aimlessly out to sea—and you will be right.

Sometimes candidates mistake an undirected style of interviewing for lack of preparation on the interviewer's part. Interviewers sometimes do fail to prepare adequately and wind up using open-ended questions to fish for material to pursue further. More likely, however, your interviewer is deliberately shifting power, responsibility, and control to you to see how you handle them. If you feel uncomfortable on the one hand or become overbearing on the other, you will fail the test.

Discomfort may reveal itself by a candidate's repeatedly asking that the interviewer clarify or narrow open questions or by giving very short answers that lack specificity. Conversely, the overbearing candidate will dominate the interview, showing little sensitivity to the interviewer's degree of interest in answers. Overbearing candidates often fail to listen closely to questions or attend to the interviewer's nonverbal communications; as a result, his or her answers are likely to be unresponsive to the interviewer's underlying concerns or attention span.

In general, you should seek clarification or narrowing of an open question only if you truly do not understand it. When an interviewer asks you to "Tell me a little about yourself" it is not a good idea to respond with, "Well, what would you like to know?" If the interviewer wanted to ask a more specific question, he or she could certainly have done so. What interviewers want to see if they ask open questions is: (1) how you will handle the opportunity to shape the interview, (2) what you think most significant about yourself, and (3) whether you have done enough homework to know what would or would not be relevant information about yourself, given the organization's needs. If you immediately turn the question back to the interviewer, you will be indicating discomfort with responsibility, an inability to recognize and take advantage of opportunities, or a lack of preparation.

On the other hand, you should not talk on and on, trying to cram all relevant information about yourself into the answer to a single question. Open questions are challenging in part because you never know when you have answered them adequately. How much or how little does the interviewer really want to know when asking you to tell a little about yourself? Does he or she expect an outline of your entire career or an answer that focuses on your most recent work experience or a reply that indicates why you are looking for work at this particular organization? Rather than tying yourself into knots with such concerns, remember that an interview is a form of conversation. Information should flow in both directions. When you have said what you want to say in reply to an open question, stop. Tolerate several moments of silence, if necessary, to give your interviewer time to take in what you have said and formulate a reply or another question. If the interviewer wants you to elaborate on points you have made or to give different information, he or she can ask for it. You are not expected to be a mind reader, but you are expected to give your interviewer a chance to reveal what he or she has in mind so that you can respond accordingly.

The Stress Interview

A much-feared but rarely encountered interview style, the stress interview seeks to evaluate a candidate's response to intense and continuous interpersonal tension. Do you get defensive? submissive? aggressive? flustered?

panicky? Or, do you remain relatively calm, alert, responsive, and asser-tive? Not surprisingly, you are most likely to encounter stress interviews if you are seeking jobs that typically involve a great deal of daily interper-sonal stress. Stress interviews are common in organizations that prize and encourage internal competition and in fields that require you to make quick decisions in tense situations.

A stress interviewer deliberately tries to make you uncomfortable, usu-ally through nonverbal behavior and metalinguistic cues. Tough and challenging questions do not constitute a stress interview, nor does an interviewer who happens to be in a lousy mood. Although these circum-stances may be stressful for you, they do not represent stress interviews because the interviewer is not deliberately pursuing a strategy designed to evaluate your response to stress. You can often jolly a moody interviewer into a happier state of mind, but an interviewer using stress as a strategy will keep the pressure on, no matter what you say or do. So, don't feel that you are failing the test if your interviewer maintains a gruff, sarcastic, or negative approach—he or she has chosen to maintain this approach and is not responding to you personally or to what you have said.

The keys to success in stress interviews are:

- Mentally rephrasing questions to focus on informational content.
- Remaining as physically relaxed as possible.
- Taking your time before answering questions.
- Tolerating silences.
- Being assertive without becoming aggressive or defensive.

All of which are easier said than done when faced with someone who is provoking you to lose your composure. Rephrasing or paraphrasing ques-tions to yourself is always a good technique for helping you formulate focused replies, but in stress interviews this technique is absolutely cru-cial. Your aim is to respond to the informational content of a question, not the emotional packaging that surrounds and obscures it. Consider the following two questions:

"What in the world makes you think that someone with a background like yours could possibly perform adequately in this position?"

"What assets do you feel you could bring to this position?"

These may seem like completely different questions—and in terms of emotional context, they are—but both can be answered with the same information. Your first job in a stress interview is to translate questions in the first form into questions like the second. Your next job is to answer them without responding in kind to the interviewer's affect, which is communicated by the phrasing of the question, tone of voice, facial expression, gestures, and posture (the nonverbal behavior and metalinguistic cues mentioned earlier). This is a tough assignment when you face a talented stress interviewer, who may make liberal use of tactics like gazing distractedly at a newspaper as you answer, tapping a pencil on the desk, yawning, looking incredulous, interrupting, staring at you intensely with arms tightly folded across chest, or greeting your answers with protracted silences.

Faced with a question like the first one listed above, take your time and reformulate the question. Then breathe from the diaphragm to give your voice adequate support and calmly begin: "I think I can do superior work in this position because I can bring to it. . . ." Maintain comfortable eye contact, regardless of what your interviewer is doing or where he or she is looking as you speak. In normal conversational interactions, speakers tend to look directly at listeners somewhere between 25 and 50 percent of the time, while listeners will maintain more intense eye contact, averaging somewhere between 60 percent and 85 percent of the time. Don't avoid looking at the interviewer, but don't try to look him or her in the eye constantly. Act normal, no matter how abnormally offensive the interviewer may be acting. It helps to remember that the interviewer is *acting*, not displaying his or her true feelings toward you as an individual.

Silence is an extremely powerful form of communication among humans. Many people find long conversational pauses almost unbearable and will blurt out anything to break them. The stress interviewer will take advantage of this tendency and try to make you uncomfortable by remaining silent for long periods. Avoid responding to silence in a stress interview—or in any other kind of interview—by filling the pause with things you did not intend to say. Breathe deeply, shift your posture without fidgeting, count to 10 or 20 or 30. When you refocus yourself and feel certain that you are not simply responding to the pressure of silence, you may supply additional information or pose a question from your agenda.

The Combination Interview

Most good interviewers will use a mix of strategies and kinds of questions in the course of an interview. A common interviewing pattern is to begin with a friendly greeting designed to put you at ease, followed by a few open-ended questions designed to get a general impression of you and your style. Based on information you supply in response to the open-ended questions, the interviewer will ask more specific, focused, or challenging questions. He or she may then use a few provocative questions and adopt selected stress tactics to test your mettle. Finally, the interviewer may turn the interaction over to you by asking whether you have any questions. Sometimes the pattern will be reversed: an interviewer may begin by asking what questions you have, saving his or her own questions until later.

Combination interviews generally reveal the most about a candidate and usually require the most preparation on the part of the interviewer. Frequently, therefore, the combination interview will take the form of a series of interviews with different individuals who will meet afterwards to pool their information and impressions. Each interviewer in the series may be assigned a different interviewing strategy. One may give you a fairly directed interview, while a second gives you an undirected interview and a third gives you the stress treatment. If you master the strategies discussed in the above sections and remain open to signals from your interviewer(s), combination interviewers should pose few problems.

The Board Interview

In a board interview, you are outnumbered. Two, three, or more interviewers meet with you at the same time, and you must respond to them individually and collectively. In some respects board interviews are the most challenging interviews because they require you to be sensitive to several people at once and to observe how they interact with one another as well as with you. Sometimes your interviewers will meet and plan an interviewing strategy beforehand, and each person will have a particular role to play. Clients frequently report running into the old good-guy–bad-guy routine, where one interviewer is open and friendly while the other is nasty or inattentive. It's a silly routine, probably born of watching too many TV versions of police interrogations, but you may run into it.

Particularly challenging are board interviews in which you meet with people from different levels of the organizational hierarchy in a single session. The conventional wisdom in such situations is to identify the major decision maker and gear your answers primarily to that person. In fact, however, identifying the major decision maker is often problematic. He or she is not necessarily the highest person on the corporate totem pole nor the most dominant person in the room. Sometimes the highest ranking person will have only veto power. He or she can say "no" to candidates but otherwise remains apart from the selection process, which means that a "yes" must come from others in the room. In some cases, each person in the room will have an implicit veto, which means that two out of three people can rate you number one in a field of candidates (including the boss) but you can still be knocked out of the race if one person takes strong exception to your selection.

The best way to handle board interviews is to treat everyone equally. Include everyone in your eye contact when you answer questions and treat questions with equal seriousness, regardless of the source. Do not play up to the boss or defer to him or her. Try to remember the names of everyone in the room, and refer to each occasionally by name, but don't overdo it. When you have opportunities to ask questions, again try to include everyone, addressing one or more questions to each if you can, or asking each to comment on the same topic, when appropriate.

THE NONVERBAL INTERVIEW

In a sense, your interview begins as soon as you walk into an organization. Before you are asked a single question, your manner, appearance, and behavior will have an impact on the people you meet. In addition, throughout the interview, your nonverbal communications as well as your words will leave their mark. In fact, studies suggest that over 80 percent of the impact you have on other people stems from nonverbal sources, rather than from the words you say.

Time

One of your first means of communicating nonverbally in interviews is by your arrival time. We in the United States are extremely sensitive to time signals: we hate to be kept waiting and are deeply offended when we feel others are wasting our time. In many other cultures, appointment times are viewed flexibly and business interactions are routinely preceded by lengthy sociable interactions. You might annoy a South American business person, for example, by insisting that a meeting start on time and by immediately launching into your business agenda. The opposite tends to be true in the United States. Also, we routinely play out status struggles through time games: if I want to tell you I'm hot and you're not, I may keep you waiting outside my office or put you on hold for several minutes in the middle of a phone conversation.

You may well run into some of these games as you interview, but take them in stride. Always aim to arrive 5 to 10 minutes early. This interval will allow you to check out the setting and give you time to compose yourself before the start of the interview. If you are unfamiliar with the area in which the organization is located, you may want to travel to the site and get your bearings before the day of the interview so that you do not have to search anxiously for the right place just before the interview.

Wait patiently for your interviewer, but not to the point of excessive self-effacement. Be willing to wait up to a half hour to interview with an individual and make sure he or she knows you have arrived before you begin your countdown. When you reach the 30-minute cutoff, politely inform the secretary, receptionist, or assistant that you are sorry you must leave because you are eager to talk with Mr. or Ms. Late. There is no need to explain why you must go. See if you can reschedule on the spot; if not, set a time to call about another appointment. This move may seem risky, but it actually communicates your sense of self-worth and generally pays off. Frequently your interviewer will be apologetic and eager to re-schedule, which shifts the power in your direction. You must, of course, use some discretion when applying the 30-minute rule. Sometimes delays are unavoidable, and sometimes you may prefer waiting to re-scheduling, especially if you are interviewing relatively far from your home base.

As you decide how to handle a particular situation, however, bear in mind that relatively few delays of over 30 minutes are truly unavoidable. Also, remember the cultural norms governing time use in the United States: willingness to wait indefinitely will implicitly put you in a one-down position, which is not the place from which you want to begin your bid for employment. Finally, consider the impact on your performance of spending more than a half hour in anxious anticipation. Waiting under such circumstances can be exhausting and can impair your self-pre-sentation.

Your handling of time during the interview is also important. You should be willing to spend a short period on small talk, taking cues from the interviewer. If your interviewer wants to get immediately down to business, follow suit. If, on the other hand, your interviewer seems will-ing to pursue small talk indefinitely, shift smoothly into your agenda as soon as you comfortably can. Remember that you have a limited amount of time and that you want to communicate your eagerness to talk about work. As the interview draws to a close, be especially sensitive to cues that signal your interviewer's desire to bring the session to an end. Do not try to prolong the interview, unless you have something very important to say and can say it briefly.

Artifacts

Anything you put on your body or carry into the interview with you is termed an *artifact* in the lingo of nonverbal communications. Clothes, jewelry, accessories, perfume, and hair style are all artifacts, and artifacts tend to be very articulate. Humans respond strongly to artifacts, which is the reason we spend so much time and money on them. You need not, however, make a fetish of them—you do not have to go out and buy a $500 briefcase to go on a job interview.

A good rule of thumb concerning dressing for interviews is to select clothes slightly more dressy than the everyday norm for the organization. If people hang out in T-shirts and dungarees, go to the interview in a pressed shirt and slacks or a skirt and blouse. If they wear slacks and sports jackets, go in a business suit or a dress and blazer. Try out your outfit before the interview if it is new; new clothes have a tendency to behave in unexpected ways. Shoes that felt comfortable in the store may give you blisters after walking a few blocks on pavement. Hemlines that seemed attractive as you stood in front of a full-length mirror may sit uncomfortably close to your navel when you seat yourself for an interview.

Keep jewelry on the conservative side and make sure your shoes are polished and clean. Stick to relatively conservative colors and patterns, especially if you are male. Don't overdo the cologne or perfume. Avoid dragging luggage into interviews—women especially are prone to come with hands and arms burdened. I've seen women come into interviews juggling a briefcase, a large shoulder bag, a coat draped over one arm, an umbrella, and a portfolio for taking notes. Then, they must search nervously for somewhere to ditch most of these accessories and spend awkward minutes searching through them to find a copy of their résumé. Take a briefcase or a bag or a portfolio, not all three.

Above all, however, dress in a way that makes you feel confident about your appearance. There is really no need to agonize about dress or to read tons of books on the topic: there are more productive ways to spend your preparation time. As long as you look neat and appropriately attired and feel comfortable with your artifacts, you will do fine.

Gestures, Postures, and Movement

When tense, many people freeze up physically. Others have been taught that gesturing or a relaxed posture is improper in formal or business settings. As noted earlier, however, gestural fluency and verbal fluency go hand in hand. Muted gestures and a rigid posture will actually make talking more difficult for you. In addition, gestures and movement enable you to command more space, and command of space is interpreted as power in our culture. Conversely, when nervous, some people gesture more, releasing tension through largely meaningless movements. This extreme, like freezing up, should be avoided.

The best approach is, again, to act naturally. Virtually everyone gestures in normal, relaxed conversation, although the amount and kind of gesturing varies depending on cultural background. But everyone gestures, and the best way to prepare for acting naturally is to get a sense of your natural gesturing patterns and those of others. Begin to observe yourself and your friends in conversation and note how and how much you and they gesture. In interviews you should try to duplicate your natural patterns, unless these patterns are distracting.

Appropriate gestures are meaningful. They emphasize, qualify, or illustrate the words they accompany. For example, if you say you have three major reasons for wanting to work at ABC, Inc., you might count off your three points using your hands and fingers. If you are saying that it took a long time to accomplish a goal, you might emphasize and illustrate "long" by holding your hands in front of your torso some distance apart. If you gesture continuously, your gestures will lose their emphatic power. On the other hand, gestures may become too emphatic, appearing to be intrusive and aggressive. A wagging finger or a handshake that crushes can create a bad impression.

Most interviews open and close with handshakes, so your handshake contributes significantly to the overall impression you make. In addition, humans respond to physical contact—touching—very strongly. A good handshake is neither limp nor overbearing. It is definite, not reluctant, and relatively brief. It may seem silly to practice your handshake, but I strongly recommend that you try out your hand on friends and ask for feedback before you start interviewing. If you are foreign born or grew up in a cultural ghetto, practice with natives—like all gestures, handshakes vary significantly from culture to culture.

To gesture freely and to look alert without seeming anxious, you need to maintain a good seating posture. You should neither sit on the edge of your chair nor lounge in it. When you first seat yourself, aim to get your buttocks firmly at the back of your chair, which will leave your torso free to move and your arms free to gesture while giving support to your back. And watch those legs. Legs crossed at the knees or ankles are fine. Hooking your ankle over your knee is not so hot—men beware. Women are rarely tempted to sit this way when attired in a dress or skirt, but many men adopt this posture immediately and may unwittingly give offense when doing so. Your leg is a formidable barrier and you don't want to put it between you and your interviewer. Also, you want to avoid the temptation to lean on your leg and play with your pants. Picking nits or playing with socks are not meaningful gestures, and if you busy your hands this way, they won't be available for more appropriate gestures.

Do not be afraid to move during the interview, as long as you do not fidget or move intrusively in someone else's space. When you move, move with confidence. Enter the room shoulders squared, head up, and treading firmly. Do not shuffle or appear to apologize with your body for taking up space. Some people have a curiously strong inclination to play with items on interviewers' desks or shelves. Stifle this inclination if you are prone to it: I've heard a surprisingly large number of interviewers complain of such behavior, which they experience as roughly equivalent to trespassing.

When in doubt about appropriate nonverbal communications, try to mirror your interviewer. When feeling in rapport, humans naturally mirror each other's posture, gestures, and movements. Observing two people in friendly conversation, it is not unusual to see both with their legs crossed the same way and their hands in roughly the same attitude. When people feel defensive or uncomfortable with one another, however, mirroring generally stops. One person may sit with hand covering mouth while the other gestures frantically; one may sit in a lounging position with both feet on the floor and legs spread widely while the other sits rigidly with legs tightly crossed. If you pick up such discrepancies, you may want to adjust your behavior.

Your voice is also part of your nonverbal self. Your words, of course, convey meaning, but so does your tone of voice, pace of speech, amount of inflection, use of vocalized pausing, and volume. Vocalized pauses are the ums, ahs, you know's, OK's, and other meaningless sounds or phrases that may fill the gaps between meaningful utterances. You should avoid peppering your speech with them, but you may use them without being aware of doing so. Eliminating them can, therefore, be difficult. If you try to become aware of and eliminate vocalized pauses only when you go for interviews, chances are good that you will only become more self-conscious, which is likely to increase your nervousness and your inclination to vocalize pauses. Try, instead, to become more conscious of your speech patterns outside and before interviews. Ask friends, for example, to point out your umming and OKing in everyday conversation and work on improvement during everyday speech. Think of yourself as replacing vocalized pauses with brief silences and get accustomed to tolerating silences, both in others and in yourself.

Practice sessions with videotape are an invaluable tool in preparing for the nonverbal as well as the verbal aspects of interviewing. Videotaping allows you to see and hear yourself much as others do and enables you to fine-tune your performance. Ideally, you should practice with an experienced coach. Sometimes, however, they are hard to find or very expensive because they work primarily with high-level executives being trained for TV appearances and the like. Communications counselors often provide coaching; as noted in Chapter 4, you can often find good coaches by calling a university-affiliated business school in your area and asking for a referral from someone in the management communications department. Before you engage a coach, however, make sure that he or she uses videotaping as a tool.

AFTER THE INTERVIEW

Your work as an interviewee does not stop at the end of an interview. Get into the habit of reviewing your performance systematically after each interview. Also, make a practice of following up after interviews with thank-you notes.

Figure 10 shows a sample self-evaluation form useful after interviews. Keeping track of your performance through systematic self-evaluation gives you feedback, which in turn enables you to improve your performance continuously. In addition, having a standard means of reviewing interviews can help you avoid the time-consuming, unproductive, and demoralizing tendency to engage in open-ended, undirected self-criticism. Don't berate yourself; improve yourself instead. Evaluate your performance dispassionately, with the goal of improving at least one aspect of your interviewing technique before the next interview.

FIGURE 10
Job Interview Evaluation Sheet

Date:

Company:

Interviewer:

Type of interview: directed, non-directed, combo, board, stress

Position:

		Thorough				Inadequate

I.   PREPARATION
    A. Knowledge of company and industry   5   4   3   2   1
    B. Knowledge of position   5   4   3   2   1
    C. Knowledge of self*   5   4   3   2   1

II. FLEXIBILITY
    A.   Success in pacing and directing responses: in revealing a substantial amount of positive information about self.
          Highly effective   Ineffective
          5   4   3   2   1
    B.   Success in adapting to the style and mood of the interviewer.
          Very successful   Not successful
          5   4   3   2   1
    C.   Ability to relate personal characteristics and previous experience to the position for which interviewing.
          Very successful   Not successful
          5   4   3   2   1

III. ENTHUSIASM
    A.   Effectiveness in demonstrating enthusiasm for industry, company, and position.
          Highly effective   Ineffective
          5   4   3   2   1

IV. LEVEL OF ANXIETY
    A.   During the interview, I felt:
          Little anxiety   Severe anxiety
          5   4   3   2   1

TOTAL SCORE FOR INTERVIEW (40 is the highest possible score)

Describe your best moment during the interview:

Describe your worst moment during the interview:

_____

_____

Follow-up indicated:
  a. When and how will you hear from the company about the results of the
      interview? _____

      _____

      _____

  b. Whom should you contact if you want additional information? _____

      _____

  c. Do you think you should send a follow-up letter or additional information
      about yourself? Yes_____   No_____
  d. If you answer "yes" to c, record date on which letter sent. _____

      _____

---

*Knowledge of what motivates you, what organizational and interpersonal setting you prefer,
what career paths appeal to you. Ability to identify major assets and liabilities.

Following up after interviews is a frequently neglected means of keeping yourself in potential employers' minds. You will stand out from other
interviewees if you take a few moments to compose a brief but personal
thank-you note. Longer follow-up letters can also give you an opportunity
to emphasize points made during an interview, to reassure your interviewer on issues of concern, or to mention information not covered in the
interview. One cautionary note. If you saw several interviewers during a
single visit, resist the temptation to compose a form letter for mass distri-
bution. Interviewers generally compare impressions, and I've known people to be rejected in the final stages of call-back interviewing because they
did not take the time to compose personal notes. Rather than take this
risk, compose a single letter for the person who serves as your major
contact in the organization. In your note, ask him or her to extend your
greetings and thanks to other members of the interviewing team.

At the end of the interview, if not before, try to get information about
the decision-making process and the next step. Ask how and when a deci-

sion will be reached so that you can better gauge what follow-up might be appropriate. If you are told, for example, that the organization expects to make a final decision within the next two weeks, ask if you might call at the end of two weeks if you have not already gotten word. Don't be afraid of seeming too pushy—you are simply demonstrating your professionalism and eagerness to work for the organization when you make provisions for following up. Diffidence is no asset when you are hunting for jobs.

Chapter Seven

After the Offers

Home free!—or are you? Your job search does not end when you receive one or more exciting offers. It's not over until you have agreed on the terms of employment, accepted a job, thanked all those who have taken time to interview you or help you in your search (including organizations that turned you down), and gracefully declined other offers.

NEGOTIATING THE TERMS OF EMPLOYMENT

Knowledge and negotiating skills are your major tools for forging a solid employment contract. You can lose literally thousands of dollars in the last few minutes of your job quest if you fail to take advantage of them.

Knowledge

You should know two things before you start negotiating the terms of employment:

1. The average salary range in the industry for the work you will be doing.
2. Your own minimum requirements.

You should have developed a firm knowledge of both through your research and self-exploration. When you have a specific offer to consider, however, you might want to take your salary research a step further. The kind of research outlined in Chapter 4 will provide you with a general idea of salary ranges appropriate to your position. But you will probably have uncovered a relatively wide range, and you may now want to narrow that range to determine what is reasonable for the geographical area, kind of organization, and level of responsibility of the particular jobs you are considering. Salary ranges for systems analysts, for example, vary widely depending on the size of the organization, the kind of organization, the complexity of its systems, the managerial responsibilities that may be involved, and the analyst's prior experience. A systems analyst with two years of experience in the field who is working for a university in the Southwest can expect to earn considerably less than a systems analyst with five years of experience working for an international bank in the Northeast. The titles of the positions may be the same, as may the formal descriptions of duties and responsibilities, yet typical salary ranges will differ significantly.

One of the best ways to get the more specific information you now seek is to get on the telephone. Pick from 4 to 10 organizations similar to the one whose offer you are considering in the geographical area where the position is located. If your offer is for a position as senior financial analyst at a large insurance company headquartered in northern New Jersey, for example, check the New York City and Northern New Jersey yellow pages under insurance. You will find many pages of listings. Pick several companies, call their switchboards and ask to speak with someone in the appropriate department.

When you've gotten into the right department, ask to speak to one of the senior analysts. Explain to him or her that you are evaluating a job offer and want to get a sense of how much people in comparable positions at other companies are being paid. Promise to share the information you gather, which will be helpful to the person at the other end of the line the next time he or she is negotiating a raise. You may get some refusals, but most people will be eager to help because the information you gather will be valuable to them, too. Inquire also about benefits, bonuses, and perks, which can amount to half or more of your salary in many positions. Once you have collected your information, prepare a short report on the results for the people who supplied the information.

Networking contacts, particularly those associated with professional organizations, can also help you narrow your sense of an appropriate range for the specific kind of position you are being offered. Use the technique outlined above, being sure to follow through on your promise to share information.

Negotiating Skills

Negotiating is a game. Some writers on the topic of negotiating refer to *win/win* situations, claiming that the proper aim of the negotiating process is to reach an agreement that is just, fair, and benefit-maximizing to all by identifying common ground and mutual interests. This claim is great in theory and may well describe how negotiating should be approached in an ideal world. Unfortunately, we do not live in an ideal world. In the real world of organizations, negotiations are almost invariably treated as games, and games are played to be won, not to reach a fair and mutually satisfying outcome.

Games are interactions with the following characteristics:

1. One or more of the individuals involved is role-playing. When playing games, we assume roles that do not represent or express our true selves—our individual beliefs, feelings, thoughts, and values. The tackle in a football game does not necessarily bear any personal animosity toward the players from the opposing team he attacks. His aggression is determined by his role, not by his personal inclinations. Likewise, he may behave cooperatively and nonaggressively toward members of his own team whom he despises. Again, his behavior is determined by his role as a team member, not by his feelings.

2. The aim of the interaction is to win the game or to gain as much as possible, not to uphold truth, justice, or the American Way. In games, rules carry far more weight than fairness or justice. When playing Monopoly, we go to "jail" when the rules of the game dictate incarceration, not when we have done something deserving of punishment. Other players will rejoice at our misfortune because it increases their chances of winning, not because they believe we deserved our fate. Game players are eager to win, even when they have nothing real at stake. No real money or benefits will accrue to Monopoly players, regardless of the outcome of the game; still, they will play vigorously to win. (The only winner in real terms when we play Monopoly is the company that makes the game.)

3. The interaction proceeds by turn taking and by allowable moves and countermoves. In a game, you make a move when, by definition according to the rules of the game, it is your turn to move. You can take a turn at play only when the rules say you can, not when you spontaneously feel inspired to participate. Furthermore, when it's your turn to play, your moves are restricted by the rules; again, you cannot simply do what you are inclined to do at the moment. A chess player cannot move his or her rook anywhere on the board; a tennis player cannot serve from anywhere on the court; a football player cannot run anywhere on the field any time he wants.

4. The moves permissible in a game are not dictated by logic, reason, fairness, or the characteristics of a particular situation. They are dictated by the rules, which the players themselves generally do not make or explicitly agree upon at the outset of play but take as givens. After hitting a home run, a baseball player must run around the bases and touch each, even though doing so makes little sense because the outcome is predetermined. Players who challenge the rules in the middle of play are likely to be thrown out of the game or severely penalized. To some extent, players are allowed to question the application of a rule to a given situation, but not the rule itself.

Playing organizational and interpersonal games is more complex than playing the games used as examples above. Most of the rules of organizational and interpersonal game playing are implicit, whereas the rules of football, chess, tennis, baseball, and Monopoly are explicit and can be explicitly cited when disputes or questions arise. In addition, the fact that an interpersonal or organizational game is being played is generally implicit and is often explicitly denied. You know when you are playing tennis or Monopoly, but you can be in the middle of interpersonal or organizational game playing without knowing that a game is in progress, much less which game.

You will be most successful in negotiating the terms of employment if you recognize that you are engaged in a game and play it to win.

Timing.   Timing is critical in games; knowledge and skill are worthless unless they can be applied at the appropriate moments. In the context of job searches, *the appropriate time to talk money is after you have been offered a job.* You will undoubtedly run into organizations and interviewers who want to start talking about salary at or near the beginning of your dealings with them. Resist the pressure firmly but politely and with a sense of humor, if possible.

Some organizations ask for a detailed salary history in their advertisements for positions. If you run into such a demand, either disregard it or cross the organization off your list. There is absolutely no valid reason to ask for this information from applicants, particularly before they have even become candidates for a job. Your salary history says nothing about your potential value to an organization, and prospective employers are in no position to evaluate the significance of your salary history in other organizations as an indicator of performance or career advancement. If the organization's goal is merely to screen candidates whose salary expectations may be out of its range, the most obvious and simple means of doing so is to include a salary range in the advertisement. If an organization wants to develop a more accurate picture of appropriate salaries for a newly created position, it should get information by the same means you used—do a little research with standard information sources and over the phone.

More likely, the organization's goal is to get someone as cheaply as possible—their demand is a move in a game. If you come across such a demand in an advertisement and find the position so appealing that you want to apply for it anyway, indicate in your cover letter your willingness to discuss the issue of salary *after* you have become a candidate for the position. If you are subsequently invited for an interview, treat the salary question as suggested in the following paragraphs—just as you would for other organizations.

When you are asked about salary expectations early in the selection-interviewing process, there are many tactics for delaying the discussion. One of them is to simply smile and ask whether you are being offered the job. If necessary, you can follow your question with a statement like, "I'd really like to learn more about the work I can do for you at this point; I'm sure we can agree on a fair salary later if we agree there's a good fit between your needs and my abilities." Or you can smile and reply, "I have no upper limits; what are yours?" Which brings us to another principle of employment negotiations: *get the interviewer to mention a figure first.* If you go first, you will be proceeding in the dark and stand a good chance of either naming a figure well below the upper limit or so far above it that you will be crossed off the list. A salary range named at this point is still open to negotiation, so you do not lock yourself into anything by continuing to pursue the job, even if the range mentioned initially is unacceptable.

Even when the interviewer mentions an appealing salary early in the selection process, defer further discussion until after you have received an offer. A committed buyer—one who has already made up his or her mind and is committed to a particular product—is less sensitive to price than the shopper who has not yet made any commitment. When you are at the top of the candidate list—when you are being offered the job—you are in a much better position to negotiate than in the early phases of the selection process. In the early stages of selection interviewing, the organization may feel no more committed to you than to a dozen other candidates; if someone comes along who looks like a real bargain, your premature indication of an acceptable salary range may cost you an offer.

After an interviewer has named a range, you may want to reveal the results of your research. You might say, for example, "Well, that seems below the norm for the industry, but I'm very interested in working for ABC and I'm certain we can reach a fair employment agreement if and when you offer me a position. So, lets keep talking about your needs and talk money later." Or, if the interviewer mentions an appealing range, you might say, "That seems a reasonable range in light of my research, but right now I'm much more interested in talking about the job than about money: I'm certain you will offer me a fair salary if we all agree I'm the right person for the work you need to have done."

Moves and countermoves.   Remember that games involve turn taking. After the other player or team makes a move, you always have an opportunity for a countermove—until the very end of the game. If a disappointing salary is named and you are told, "This is absolutely as high as we can go," keep in mind that you have not yet reached the end of the game—the ball is simply in your court and you have the next turn. Taking time out is a move allowable in almost every game, and after an offer has been made, calling for time out is generally a good move.

In *How to Make $1000 a Minute*,[1] Jack Chapman recommends responding enthusiastically to the offer, but not accepting the job at this point. He suggests asking for the offer in writing by saying something on the order of, "That sounds good to me. Would you write it down and mail me a copy so we're both certain we're clear? I'll get back to you on it as soon as you need to have an answer. What time frame would be good for you?" Conveying enthusiasm for the job and the organization is crucial when making such a request, as is displaying sensitivity to the organization's needs. You do not want to appear to be hesitant about the desirability of the job.

Rarely will you be met with a demand for an instant decision. Players in organizational games don't want to appear to be bad sports or dirty players (often they don't want to appear to be playing a game at all). In a selection process that has spanned several weeks or months, demanding an on-the-spot decision—especially after a perfectly reasonable and highly professional request to have an offer in writing—would strike anyone as foul play.

In the time you have gained, consider the offer, your options, and your needs carefully. Remember that salary is only one aspect of a total employment agreement, so be sure to consider the whole package before reaching a decision. If you feel the offer is unacceptable, you might as

---

[1]Jack Chapman, *How to Make $1000 a Minute* (Berkeley, Calif.: Ten Speed Press, 1987).

well take a last stab at getting an increase. Call and reiterate your enthusiasm for the company and the work and your certainty that you would be a good investment for the organization. Then explain why you cannot afford to accept the offer and ask whether there is any possibility of the organization coming up to $_____. If the original offer is truly unacceptable, you have absolutely nothing to lose because the worst that can happen is that the offer will be withdrawn, which is no loss if you intended to reject it anyway.

It is highly likely that after calm consideration, the offer will not seem totally unacceptable, unless you have other, better salary offers in hand. It will still seem disappointing, but you still have a turn coming, and you are in a relatively strong position because the organization has shown its desire to employ you, while you have not yet shown a comparable degree of commitment.

A good rule to observe in negotiating games is not give ground on a point without getting something in return. If you agree to a salary below the minimum of your range, you are making a concession and it is appropriate to seek a concession in return. If you play the game well, you may actually be able to win concessions that will be worth more to you in the long run than a higher salary. As noted above, salary is only one aspect of a complete employment agreement. As you evaluate an offer and prepare for further negotiations, consider asking for concessions in the perks and benefits listed below, and use your imagination in figuring out how you can use them to substantially increase the value of the offer:

- Bonuses and commissions
- Use of company cars
- Insurance
- Expense accounts
- Tuition remission
- Opportunities for in-house training
- Severance pay and benefits
- Health club memberships and corporate dining privileges
- Possibilities for promotion and advancement
- Timing of performance reviews
- Payment of fees for professional memberships and subscriptions to journals
- Vacation time and provisions for leaves of absence

- Child care
- Pension plans
- Stock options
- Relocation expenses

Negotiating a performance and salary review every six months instead of a year gives you twice as many opportunities for raises. Sometimes you can win an automatic pay raise, providing your performance is good. In your first year of employment alone, this move can net you several thousand dollars.

Stock options—or any sort of equity in exchange for your work—are often more affordable to organizations than cash, especially when cash flow is low. Equity can offer you a high return over the years, and you may be able to win it cheaply from an organization that cannot afford a higher salary.

If you have decided to return to school, tuition payments have a high value. Negotiate the organization's complete support of your endeavors, including time off to attend classes, work on projects, and take tests. Get a promise of flexibility in your scheduling.

Go through the list and make sure you know what you are being offered in addition to salary. If you receive a salary offer below your minimum, calculate what it would take in terms of other benefits to make up the difference—in other words, ask yourself what it would take to make the offer attractive. Also, identify fall-back positions. If a firm's policy is to make equity opportunities available only to partners, you might ask to have your eligibility for partnership reviewed earlier than usual. If you want a larger commission on sales and they refuse, you might ask for a higher commission only on sales over a certain value. Remember: each time you concede a point, you are going to try to win a concession in return.

When you get back to the organization about its offer, make a counterproposal—a counter move. Ask for more than your minimum to give yourself room for further negotiating and to maximize your yield. *Successful negotiators start out high, rather than from a "reasonable" or moderate position.* To a large extent, the more you ask for, the more you are likely to receive. But avoid patently unreasonable positions. You will have to justify your position in terms of benefits to the company. The name of the game the organization plays is "Let's make a profit" (even not-for-profits must generate enough resources from hiring you to at least cover what you cost), so your most convincing argument for increased compensation will be a higher return to the organization. Appeals to fairness or need will not get you very far in this game, no matter how valid or justified they might be outside the context of the game. You will get further if you play by the rules.

Knowing when to end the game is also important in negotiating. Sometimes, even if you could get more by pushing, you are better off accepting somewhat less and maintaining good will. Face saving is, I expect, more important in our gaming culture than is generally recognized. Pushing the other person to a humiliating defeat only breeds resentment and a desire for revenge. The people with whom you are playing the negotiating game are individuals separate from the organization, as well as its representatives; the organization will not lose face or feel humiliated, but they may. Their stake in the game is nonmaterial because they are not playing with their own resources (unless, of course, you are talking to business owners). Their stake is psychological—just as in the case of Monopoly players—and you may sacrifice their good will if you leave them feeling totally defeated. This is what win/win negotiating is really about—leaving all players feeling that they have benefited or at least that they have not lost on all fronts—not about reaching a fair, just, or benefit-maximizing agreement.

After you have agreed on an offer, put it in writing. In addition to your oral acceptance, write a letter of acceptance that outlines the terms of the agreement, especially those points that are nonstandard. For example, if the organization has agreed to support your educational endeavors with time off and flexible scheduling, note this in your letter. The goal is to strengthen and clarify the organization's commitments to you and yours to it. Oral agreements have a way of being forgotten or of being recalled differently by different parties. Your letter will be helpful if a question ever arises concerning any unusual or nonstandard terms of your employment.

A client of mine once related the following story. She had secured an oral agreement from her prospective boss that if she became pregnant she could take up to four months unpaid leave, in addition to the three months paid leave the company traditionally provided. The boss left the company six months after she started working, and when the question of leave came up, her new boss insisted that she stick to the time normally allotted. He said he would not and could not be bound by any private understandings she had reached with his predecessor. Because she did not have documentation to prove that additional leave was one of the terms of her employment, her new boss treated it as a personal favor, and refused to be bound by it. So, don't relax as soon as you have accepted an offer; take the time to make sure both you and the organization clearly understand of what the offer consists.

Dealing with multiple possibilities.   Since you have been prospecting and interviewing continually throughout your search, an offer is likely to arrive from one or more organizations while you are still interviewing or negotiating with others. If these other possibilities still appeal, you will want time to pursue them further. What do you do, however, if the organization that made you an offer wants a reply before the other possibilities ripen? First, try to get an extended time out. Greet the offer with enthusiasm and acknowledge the organization's eagerness to take you on. But add that it is important at this point in your career to make a sound decision and that you would like a couple of weeks to consider it. Sometimes your request will be granted, sometimes it won't. You will usually be able to buy some time but often not as much as you would like.

Use whatever time you can get to work on moving those other possibilities toward definite offers. Explain to your contacts in other organizations that you have received an offer and must make a decision by _____. Ask their help in moving the selection process along. You must, of course, communicate the sense that you are very interested in working for them and would very likely accept an offer, if one were made. If this fails and you are caught between the demand for a decision from one organization and another's inability to move forward its decision, you face a difficult choice. You have basically four options:

1. Say yes to the firm offer and withdraw from consideration at other organizations.
2. Go back to the first organization and explain your situation in hopes that they will extend the decision deadline.
3. Stall for time with the first organization; let the deadline pass silently and wait with fingers crossed for them to badger you.
4. Say yes to the offer but continue to pursue other possibilities and be prepared to quit the job if you get a more attractive offer.

Option 1 presents no problems as long as you feel good about the organization, the work, and the offer. On the other hand, you have little to lose by trying 2 and 3 before making your decision. Option 2—asking for more time—may annoy the first organization, and your request may simply not be granted, but you are not likely to lose the offer merely because you asked for more time, providing you have not already exceeded the time limit. Option 3—stalling—is usually safe, if not entirely nice or professional; an organization will generally get in touch with you before making an offer to someone else or withdrawing the offer to you. If and when the organization does get in touch, however, you will have to provide an answer at once.

Option 4 is not the best move in terms of public relations, especially if an organization has made a significant investment in you before you leave. On the other hand, if you told them before accepting their offer that you wanted more time and they pushed you to make a decision, they are as responsible as you for the losses. Organizations feel less and less loyal to their employees in these days of cutbacks and layoffs, and most have demonstrated a readiness to let people go whenever doing so is in their best interests. You should not feel obligated to stay, therefore, if it is in your best interests to go. If you decide on option 4 and do leave, try to make your departure as painless as possible for the organization by offering to help find and train a successor and to bring pending projects to a satisfactory conclusion before going. You have nothing to gain by creating an excess of ill will.

DECLINING GRACEFULLY AND PRODUCTIVELY

If you follow the advice given so far in this book, I'm certain you will have the happy problem of declining offers and withdrawing candidacies gracefully and productively. The following tips should help you:

1. Withdraw from consideration at other organizations as soon as you have accepted an offer. My advice is to let them know both by phone and by letter. This courtesy will enable you to maintain friendly contacts with people who will be valuable for future career moves and often for current business as well.

2. Over the phone, you will likely have to leave a message. In letters, explain your decision succinctly, thank interviewers for the time they have spent with you, and give your new title and business address—not necessarily in that order.

3. Go through your contacts file and create a mailing list of people you want to inform of your career or job change. Create standard paragraphs to convey the information suggested in step 2: your career decision and the reason for it, a word of thanks for help, and your current title, address, and phone number for business transactions. Make your correspondence personal by adding opening or closing paragraphs that are unique to your receiver. These short paragraphs can be handwritten.

4. Keep your contacts file active. Go through it periodically; make phone calls and write letters as needed to maintain productive communication throughout the network you have created.

IN CLOSING

Enjoy your new job or career choice. But be prepared for change: organizational loyalties are loosening, and people are changing both jobs and careers more and more frequently. A modern work life often consists of 7 to 10 jobs along 2 or 3 career paths. Vocational decision making is a lifetime activity. Use the time between occupations to communicate and to improve your communication skills; also use it to re-explore yourself and adjust your career accordingly.

Have fun and aim for happiness.

Index